Claude Schwab

HEDGE ME

Interviews
Recruiters
Resumes
Compensation

The Insider's Guide: U.S. Hedge Fund Careers

Lynx Media

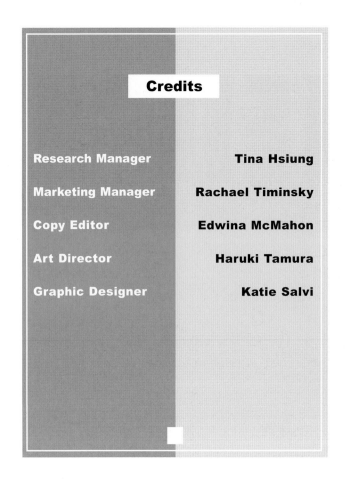

Credits

Research Manager	Tina Hsiung
Marketing Manager	Rachael Timinsky
Copy Editor	Edwina McMahon
Art Director	Haruki Tamura
Graphic Designer	Katie Salvi

For permission to reproduce selections from this report, contact Lynx Media, 244 Madison Avenue, #304, New York, NY 10016, or e-mail info@schwabenterprise.com.

Library of Congress Control Number: 2006928970

ISBN 0-9744188-5-4

Printed in the United States of America.

From the Author

I wrote *HEDGE ME* because so many aspiring hedge fund analysts and traders were finding it difficult to get precise answers to their career-related questions. The industry seems remarkably devoid of reliable industry and firm-specific information and is still too new to enable most parents, friends and family, professors, or career services staff to speak definitively on getting a hedge fund job and on hedge fund employment as a long-term career.

Many professionals—both in finance and in other fields—have many misconceptions and stereotypes about the industry. Until very recently otherwise first-rate news publications had fallen asleep at the hedge fund wheel as they churned out sensationalistic and often inaccurate stories on the industry. By mid-2005 several of these publications finally added better coverage, perhaps realizing that hedge funds were not some fad. The sensationalism ebbed somewhat, yet reporters in positions of enormous influence at leading publications continue to print factual errors on how hedge fund are run and managed, while others write of these "fiendishly complicated investment vehicles" (*The Economist*, April 2006); a "rocket science" premise that then apparently excuses reporters from critical and unbiased analysis, in favor of producing misinformation wrapped in accusatorial undertones.

I hope to have finally dispelled these inaccuracies and misrepresentations in *HEDGE ME* and show that hedge funds are investment firms run by investment managers from varied backgrounds whose intentions are no different from the goals of investment managers of decades past, namely to identify, size, and profit from discrepancies between their and the market's view on value. Their analyses can have investment horizons that are short term, medium term, or long term in nature. Meanwhile these managers are held to identical standards on securities laws relating to fraud as any other investment professional. And the only difference between hedge fund managers and other investment managers is that hedge fund managers are less restricted in the asset classes and types of strategies they can pursue, and the rewards of being right can be much greater given the incentive structure of the hedge fund business model.

The fourth edition is meant not merely to update industry data and recruiting resources from prior editions. It has been designed to be richer by incorporating a fuller discussion of the interviewing process. We have added more interviewing questions within a larger array of investment strategies to prepare as many candidates as possible for any sort of interview. We think the fourth edition of *HEDGE ME* will best prepare you to move into your exciting and challenging career in the hedge fund industry.

Table of Contents

Tables: Industry Basics

Resumes: Good Examples

FAQs: Direct Answers to Your Questions

A

INTRODUCTION

This guide has been written for experienced professionals and business students interested in hedge fund employment opportunities. It provides a realistic overview of the hedge fund industry and hedge fund careers. The guide is meant to help business professionals and students find hedge fund opportunities and prepare for interviews. It also provides guidelines for compensation.

The guide focuses on two functional roles within a hedge fund: the investment analyst or junior analyst and the trader or junior trader. The role of an investment analyst is functionally standard throughout the hedge fund industry and includes the analysis and due diligence required for investment decisions. The amount of work experience and the expected level of contribution to the investment portfolio may vary at each firm. The typical investment analyst has either earned an MBA degree and has had several years of full-time work experience between his/her undergraduate and graduate programs or has earned a college degree and has between two and three years of full-time experience in financial services or the business sector. The typical trader has earned a college degree and has two to three years of full-time experience. A junior analyst or trader is typically a recent college or university graduate with no more than one to two years of professional work experience.

There are two types of hedge fund traders, each of whom performs a distinct functional role. One is the execution trader, whose primary role is to execute investment ideas provided by the investment analyst and/or portfolio manager (PM); and the other is the trader responsible for profit and loss (P&L), whose primary role is to generate investment decisions and trading strategies. In such instances, the investment role of the trader and portfolio manager often converges. This is especially true for traders of fixed-income products who tend to conduct their own analyses.

For the purpose of this guide, however, only the execution trader will be considered, as the trader with P&L responsibilities typically has had significant public market investment or trading experience. The guide will also review the differences between investment banking, or "sell-side" execution traders, and asset management, or "buy-side" execution traders, particularly when dealing with hedge fund investment strategies that are complex and/or trading oriented **(Table 1)**.

Not covered in this guide are mid-office and back-office roles, often referred to as hedge fund infrastructure roles. They include the marketers, investor relations personnel, the chief financial officer (CFO), the chief operating officer (COO), the chief compliance officer (CCO), the chief administrative officer (CAO), the chief technology officer (CTO), and other operational personnel. Typically these roles do not differ significantly from similar functional roles at financial services and traditional asset management firms.

Other basic topics not covered in this guide but commonly found in books on job opportunities and interviewing preparatory advice are the normal preparation and etiquette expected of any interviewee during any professional interview: for example, arrive on time. And when in doubt regarding proper attire, always err on the side of the formal—even though hedge fund personnel in general tend to dress casually. And display a high level of energy, intensity, and interest in the opportunity, and never give the impression of resting on the laurels of accomplishments or successes. In the case of hedge fund interviews, the interviewer should feel the candidate's hunger to trade or to spend day after day listening to company management conference calls, attending industry conferences, building investment models, dissecting financial statements, and developing industry trends. For the purpose of this guide, we will assume that the candidate has already learned such general interviewing skills.

Buy Side and Sell Side   Table 1

The "buy side" refers to asset management firms that invest the capital of individuals and institutional investors. Buy-side asset managers can invest in publicly traded securities or securities of privately held firms, depending on their firm charter or partnership agreement. Private equity funds invest primarily in the securities of privately held firms. Buy-side professionals at hedge funds invest primarily in publicly traded securities and both make money through management fees (typically 1% to 3% of assets under management) and performance-based incentive fees (typically 20% of profit). Buy-side professionals at traditional asset management firms invest in publicly traded securities and typically make money through management fees only.

The "sell side" refers to the functions of an investment bank/brokerage firm. Sell-side professionals issue, recommend, trade, and sell securities for the investors on the buy-side. The sell-side can be thought of primarily as a facilitator of buy-side investments—the sell-side makes money through fees and commissions for these facilitating services. Note however that some sell-side firms do have buy-side divisions with investment professionals investing on behalf of the firm and/or firm clients.

Hedge funds are structured less formally than sell-side firms and career paths are more flexible and vary more from one firm to another.

HEDGE FUNDS

What Is a Hedge Fund?

A *hedge fund* is an investment structure designed to manage a private investment pool. It establishes a method of manager compensation, the number and types of investors, and the rights and responsibilities of those investors regarding profits, redemptions, taxes, and reports. In December 2004 the Securities and Exchange Commission (SEC) ruled that hedge funds must register with the SEC. As of February 2006 all hedge funds with assets under management greater than $30 million, with at least 15 investors and with investor capital lock-up periods of less than two years are supposed to register with the SEC under the Investment Advisors Act of 1940 and must then submit to SEC examinations. According to the SEC, more than 1000 hedge fund managers had registered by the deadline. As of June 2006, however, hedge funds' SEC registration requirements were overturned by the United States Court of Appeals for the District of Columbia. Therefore, as of the date of this publication, it remains to be seen whether hedge funds will begin to de-register.

Unlike traditional buy-side asset management firms that typically make only "long" investments, hedge funds can take advantage of both "long" and "short" investment approaches and can borrow capital to increase the size of an investment position (leverage). A *long* investment is the purchase of a security. The intention is to benefit from an increase in the price of the security. *Short selling* is borrowing a security to sell on the open market and buying it back at a later time at a lower price, it is hoped. The intention is to benefit from a decrease in the price of the security. Short positions can be taken as hedges for associated long positions or as stand-alone investments. *Hedging* involves taking a secondary position with the expressed purpose of counterbalancing a known risk involved in a primary position.

Ability	Traditional Fund	Hedge Fund
• To Short	N	Y
• To Leverage	N	Y
• To maintain concentrated cash positions	N	Y
• To maintain concentrated equity positions	N	Y
• To invest in less liquid/illiquid assets	N	Y

Unlike most traditional asset management firms, hedge funds are also allowed to maintain concentrated cash positions and can take concentrated equity positions.

Although industry experts typically use the word *alternative* to describe hedge fund investment strategies, in contrast to *traditional* investment strategies, this term is problematic, as are frameworks that attempt to separate the private equity buy side from the hedge fund buy side. Traditional asset management firms are making inroads into alternative investment strategies; meanwhile private equity firms and hedge funds are making inroads into each other's territories; some hedge funds and private equity firms are even housed under the same roof. Of course, fundamental structural differences still exist between private equity firms and hedge funds, such as investor liquidity constraints and lock-up periods, the ability of hedge funds to benefit from a decrease in the price of a security, the level of direct management control over investments afforded the private equity firm, as opposed to hedge funds that typically vote on management teams and company prospects with their long and short decisions, and the type of information available for investment decisions.

We also see hedge funds making inroads into sell-side banking/direct lending activities in their search for strong returns.

Investment Strategies

There are several ways to categorize hedge funds, and sometimes it is difficult to place a fund in one particular category. Joseph Nicholas, in his book, *Investing in Hedge Funds: Strategies for the New Marketplace*, categorizes 11 investment strategies, which are listed and briefly described on the following pages.

Investment Categories   Table 2

STRATEGIES	SUMMARY DESCRIPTION
Fixed-Income Arbitrage	Offsetting long and short positions in related but mis-priced fixed income securities and their derivatives; investor typically uses leverage to magnify small changes in relationships between the instruments
Equity Market Neutral (Statistical Arbitrage)	Approximately equal dollar amounts of offsetting long and short equity positions to profit from over-valued and undervalued stocks
Convertible Arbitrage	Long portfolios of convertible bonds hedged by selling short underlying stock of each bond; generally price of convertible falls less rapidly than that of stock in down markets and will mirror price of stock in rising markets
Merger (Risk) Arbitrage	Trying to anticipate outcome of announced merger and capture spread between current market price of the target company and the price to which it will appreciate if deal is completed. Target company typically trades at a discount as mergers take time and involve some risk
Distressed Securities	Invest in securities of companies in financial difficulties; pricing of these securities often distorted as many buyers either legally or customarily must sell troubled companies

| **Investment Categories** | **Table 2** (Continued) |

STRATEGIES	SUMMARY DESCRIPTION
Event-Driven	Significant events often occur during corporate life cycles; uncertainty about the outcomes of these events creates investment opportunities for a specialist who can correctly anticipate outcomes
Macro Investing	Top-down global approach that concentrates on forecasting how global macroeconomic and political events affect valuation of financial instruments; directional market exposure; often macro investing combined with other hedge fund strategies
Sector Specialists	Investing in group of companies or segment of the economy with a common product or market, often combining sector directional bets with hedged positions
Equity Hedge	Combined core long holdings of equities with short sales of stocks or stock index options; idea is to take long positions in stocks that will outperform the market and sell short stocks that will underperform the market
Emerging Market	Make primarily long investments in the securities of companies in countries with "emerging" financial markets. Profit by mining such markets for under-valued assets and purchasing them before market corrects itself
Short Selling	Profit from decline in the value of stocks; involves a security that the investor does not own to take advantage of an anticipated price decline

MAR/Hedge, one of the leading subscription-based newsletters on the hedge fund market-place, provides us with an example of a different fund categorization:

• **Event-driven**: includes distressed securities, risk arbitrage

• **Global**: includes focus on international market, emerging market, regional market

• **Global macro**: includes focus on changes in global economic variables

• **Market neutral**: includes convertible arbitrage, stock index arbitrage, fixed income arbitrage

• **Short seller**: includes taking position that stock prices will go down

• **U.S. (country-specific) opportunity**: includes value, growth/small cap, short-term

To understand fully what hedge fund professionals do, it is helpful to debunk some of the ingrained stereotypes surrounding them: (1) They survive from the highs of a fast-paced environment and are fully focused on short-term trading based on gossamer informational leads and weak or rushed analysis; (2) They are market-timing fanatics hooked to their Bloomberg terminals, continually reacting to the smallest bit of news with major changes in investment position; (3) They are deal loving and transactions hungry—a stereotype formerly reserved for investment bankers during active business cycles.

The truth is that some hedge fund managers do provide higher risk alternatives to traditional long-only investments, while others provide substantially lower risk alternatives. Some magnify the financial exposure to various markets, while others provide protection against market declines or neutralize certain market risks. Some provide short-term trading strategies, while others provide arbitrage opportunities, and still others provide long-term investment approaches. Finally, and perhaps most important, some hedge and some do not.

The hedge fund industry consists of numerous strategies, and within particular strategies one often finds various investment styles. Some styles are momentum based or event driven and do involve technical market timing and short-term trading based on news flow, whereas others involve long-term investment horizons and rigorous financial valuations and analysis—far exceeding the analysis performed by many sell-side analysts and investment bankers and far removed from the daily news and market pricings influencing the stock price.

Top 25 Hedge Funds

On the next page is a list of the top 25 hedge funds **(Table 3)** based on *Institutional Investor's* annual list of *Top 100 Hedge Funds*. The rankings are based on firm/fund capital. We can make three general observations based on four years of data: first, we note the emergence of financial services firms into the lineup over the past two years; second, we notice how firms/funds can experience big changes in ranking, especially as established banks enter the fray and strong performing funds amass assets quickly; and third, we see the continual drastic rise in the number of firms with assets of $5+ billion. In the 2006 rankings, 62 firms had assets in excess of $5 billion, compared to 45 in the 2005 rankings, and only 16 in the 2002 rankings. And as recently as 2003, the $10+ billion hedge funds did not exist.

Table 4 ranks cities based on their hedge fund equity assets. While it should come as no surprise

**Hedge Fund
Due Diligence**

- Inception Date
- Strategy
- Style
- Asset Class(es)
- Size
- Fund Performance
- PM Backgrounds
- Employee Turnover
- Performance Relative to Funds Strategies
- Hedging Component of Fund
- Actual Investments
- Hedge Fund Investor Base
- Number of Funds in Firm
- Organization: Industry or Generalist
- Founder(s) Motives
- Founder(s) Skill Sets

Rank 2006	Rank 2005	Rank 2004	Rank 2003	Firm/Fund name(s)	Firm/Fund capital ($ millions)	Return net of fees (%)
1	3	28	81	**Goldman Sachs Asset Mgmt** (New York, NY)	21,023	
2	2	10	49	**Bridgewater Associates** (Westport, CT)	20,886	
				Pure Alpha Strategy	20,886	3.46
3	7	22	26	**D.E. Shaw Group** (New York, NY)	19,900	
				Macro	6,500	16.7
				Equity & equity-linked strategies	5,200	14.1
				Distressed securities-related strategies	3,800	11.4
				Futures & currency-related strategies	1,300	12.1
4	1	4	4	**Farallon Capital Mgmt** (San Francisco, CA)	16,400	14
5	16	22	19	**ESL Investments** (Greenwich, CT)	15,000	
6	15	16	16	**Barclays Global Investors** (London, U.K.)	14,330	
7	9	11	9	**Och-Ziff Capital Mgmt Group** (New York, NY)	14,300	
				Och-Ziff Master	11,500	8.9
				Och-Ziff Europe	1,800	16
				Och-Ziff Asia	1,000	14.5
8	5	14	13	**Man Investments** (London, U.K.)	12,700	
				Man AHL Diversified	2,101	16.8
				Man AHL Alpha	149	14.3
				Athena Guaranteed Futures	33	14.3
9	11	12	11	**Tudor Investment Corp.** (Greenwich, CT)	12,683	
				Raptor Global Portfolio	6,284	8.89
				Tudor BVI Global Portfolio	5,274	14.67
				Witches Rock Portfolio	422	3.07
				Tudor Tensor Portfolio	385	5.44
				Tudor Futures Fund	259	14.49
10	7	1	1	**Caxton Associates** (New York, NY)	12,500	
				Caxton Global Investments, Ltd/ Caxton Global Investments (USA) LLC	10,000	8.03
				Caxton Healthcare Trading	660	2.55
				Caxton Alpha Equity	600	15.03
11	6	5	3	**Citadel Investment Group** (Chicago, IL)	12,000	
				Citadel Kensington Global Strategies	9,000	7.17
				Citadel Wellington	3,000	6.06
12	19	21	35	**Campbell & Co.** (Towson, MD)	11,500	
				Campbell Composite		11.6
				Financial, Metal and Energy (FME) Large Portfolio		11.01
				Global Diversified Large Portfolio		11.87
13	12	20	16	**Perry Capital** (New York, NY)	11,325	
				Perry Partners International	7,287	5.22
				Perry Partners LP	3,545	5.04
14	4	2	18	**GLG Partners** (London, U.K.)	11,241	
15	16	13	12	**Cerberus Capital Mgmt** (New York, NY)	11,200	
16	26	22	19	**Lone Pine Capital** (Greenwich, CT)	11,000	
				Lone Cascade		27
				Lone Cypress		32
				Lone Kauri		34
16	14	15	8	**Maverick Capital** (Dallas, TX)	11,000	

Rank 2006	Rank 2005	Rank 2004	Rank 2003	Firm/Fund name(s)	Firm/Fund capital ($ millions)	Return net of fees (%)
18	13	19	5	**Moore Capital Mgmt** (New York, NY)	10,200	
				Moore Credit		9.9
				Moore Emerging Markets		20.3
				Moore Fixed Income		15.6
				Moore Global Investments		16.2
19	20	6	6	**Angelo Gordon & Co.** (New York, NY)	10,000	
20	21	8	7	**Soros Fund Mgmt** (New York, NY)	9,600	
				Quantum Endowment Fund	9,600	12.3
21	62	93	76	**Atticus Capital** (New York, NY)	9,200	
				Atticus European		62
				Atticus Global		22
				Atticus International		21
22	23	37	-	**Brevan Howard Asset Mgmt** (London, U.K.)	8,975	
				Brevan Howard Master Fund	8,754	
23	-	-	-	**HSBC** (London, U.K.)	8,853	
				Sinopia Asset Mgmt (Paris, France)	8,278	
				HSBC Halbis Partners (London, U.K.)	575	
				HSBC European Alpha Fund	270	10.48
				HSBC Atlantic Global Opportunities Fund	114	6.77
				HSBC Multi-Strategy Arbitrage Fund	74	6.15
				HSBC Global Technology Alpha Fund	55	7.22
				HSBC Merger Arbitrage Offshore Fund	18	3.69
24	22	17	25	**JP Morgan Chase & Co.** (New York, NY)	8,826	
				Highbridge Capital Mgmt (New York, NY)	8,093	
				Highbridge Capital Corp.	5,385	5.05
				Highbridge Event Driven/ Relative Value Fund Ltd	1,215	11.64
				Highbridge Long/ Short Equity Fund	497	7.77
				Highbridge European Special Situations Fund Ltd	234	2.46
				Highbridge Asia Opportunities Fund	197	6.88
				JF Asset Mgmt (Hong Kong)	613	
				JF Japan Absolute Return Fund	353	23.5
				JF Korea Absolute Return Fund	104	21.6
				JF Asia Absolute Return Fund	85	-1.7
				JF Greater China Absolute Return Fund	42	2.1
				JF India Absolute Return Fund	12	8.51
				J.P. Morgan Alternative Asset Mgmt (New York, NY)	120	
				J.P. Morgan Absolute Return Mortgage Fund	120	
25	38	34	15	**HBK Investments** (Dallas, TX)	8,812	
				HBK Master Fund	8,812	7.62

Source: Institutional Investor's Alpha, June 2006, June 2005, and 2004 issues

that New York City leads the world in hedge fund equity assets, it is interesting to note that three of the top ten cities are based in Connecticut and nine of the top ten are in the United States.

Hedge Fund Cities **Table 4**

TOP 10 HEDGE FUND CITIES (Equity Assets)*

City	State/Country	Equity Assets ($MM)	# of Firms
New York	NY	$386,622	392
Greenwich	CT	$64,236	34
San Francisco	CA	$39,351	62
Boston	MA	$31,855	33
Chicago	IL	$30,984	17
London	UK	$22,361	60
Dallas	TX	$21,817	23
Stamford	CT	$16,529	21
Los Angeles	CA	$11,081	17
Westport	CT	$7,053	4

*Determined by Equity Assets filed by hedge fund managers in 13F Filings with the SEC in 1Q2006. Does not include Equity Assets filed by Investment Advisors.

Source: Thomson Financial

Due Diligence on a Particular Hedge Fund

Once a candidate is more comfortable with the hedge fund industry as a whole and the functional role he/she wants, it is time to gather information on particular hedge funds.

While the following sections provide primary and secondary resources for those performing due diligence on a fund, note that the industry is still somewhat opaque. The good news though is that countless portfolio managers emphasize the self-selection process for those who conduct their homework and research on a fund, using the resources listed below as well as personal networks, school alumni networks, friends, and colleagues. Many PMs are convinced that a candidate "should be able to find someone who knows someone who works at a hedge fund or knows something about the firm."

Every hedge fund has a reputation, typically dictated by the firm's history, investment style, strategy, size (assets under management, number of investment professionals), annual performance, and, perhaps most important, the character of its PM(s).

Candidates should research the style and professional background of the PMs at the firm. Sometimes simply knowing that the managing partner's name is the name of the fund embla-

Investment Returns

Table 5

Credit Suisse/Tremont Hedge Fund Index

	Total Return 2005	Total Return 2004	Total Return 2003	CAGR 5 yr.	CAGR 10 yr.	Dev* 10 yr.	Std Sharpe Ratio** 10yr.
Convertible Arbitrage Index	-2.55	1.98	12.90	5.72	9.67	4.79	1.26
Dedicated Short Bias Index	17.00	-7.72	-32.59	-5.46	-2.44	17.98	-.34
Distressed Index	11.74	15.62	25.12	13.74	13.32	6.40	1.51
Emerging Markets Index	17.39	12.49	28.75	17.02	11.01	15.20	.48
Equity Market Neutral Index	6.14	6.48	7.07	7.31	10.95	2.76	2.65
Event Driven Index	8.95	14.47	20.02	11.13	11.75	5.89	1.38
Event Driven Multi-Strategy Index	7.21	14.04	17.19	9.90	11.02	6.34	1.16
Fixed Income Arbitrage Index	.63	6.86	7.97	5.93	6.24	3.85	.67
Global Macro Index	9.25	8.4	17.99	13.85	14.23	10.33	1.02
Hedge Fund Index	7.61	9.64	15.44	9.42	11.30	7.54	1.02
Long/Short Equity Index	9.68	11.56	17.27	9.19	13.09	10.77	.88
Managed Futures Index	-.11	5.97	14.13	9.48	7.86	11.96	.35
Multi-Strategy Index	7.54	7.53	15.04	9.15	10.70	3.69	1.91
Risk Arbitrage Index	3.08	5.45	8.9	3.71	7.37	4.42	.84

Monthly standard deviation annualized.   ** *Calculated using 90-day U.S. T-bill.*

Note: Index data begins January 2005 and all of the above indices include dividends.

Note: All CAGR and Std Dev numbers are percentages (%)

Note: To qualify for the index, a fund must meet the following requirements:

- *A minimum of US $10 million assets under management*
- *A minimum one-year track record, and*
- *Current audited financial statements.*

Source: Credit Suisse/Tremont Hedge Fund Index

zoned on the front door of the offices can speak volumes about how the fund is run. Also, it is important to know what motivates the founder(s) and what their skill sets are. Some are great at managing money, others are great at managing people and building organizations, and a rare few are competent at both. Get to know the names and backgrounds of the people you might be meeting and how the analysts and traders interact with one another. If the firm experiences high employee turnover, you should try to determine why. If the firm has several funds, be familiar with each fund strategy.

It is also important to know a fund's actual investments and how and why the returns of one firm differ from another's with a similar strategy. Certain investment strategies tend to generate a certain range of returns **(Table 5)**. However, there is often a wide disparity in investment results for funds that use similar strategies due to the various styles and acumen of the firms' PM(s).

Another key fact to understand is whether the hedge fund actually hedges. This may seem like a fairly mundane question, but many hedge funds do not hedge. Simply taking long and short positions that are independent of each other is not considered hedging. If they are, in fact, hedging, how are they doing it?

Some funds hire industry generalists, and others hire industry specialists. Prior to meeting with a fund, one should make sure that the firm is run one way or the other. Some firms combine specialists and generalists.

Finally candidates should become familiar with the fund's investor base—more simply put, whose money does the manager (General partnership or GP) manage? Is it outside investor money (Limited partnership or LP) or firm partner money or both? If it is outside investor money, is it high net worth money or institutional? If it's the latter, which types of institutions invest and how fragmented is the LP base? In bad times a single withdrawal in a nonfragmented LP base can shut down a fund. It is also important to determine how "sticky" (long-term horizon) or "fast" (short-term horizon) or "smart" (level of financial sophistication) the LP money is.

FAQ 1 → What Information Resources Are Available?

The SEC prohibits hedge funds from advertising their funds or promoting themselves in the media. Consequently, conducting due diligence on a fund cannot begin with a fund's Web site.

Most hedge funds don't have Web sites that are accessible to the general public. Hedge funds can advertise only to accredited investors, as defined in the Securities Exchange Act of 1933.

Conducting due diligence on hedge funds with no external investor base is even more difficult to obtain. Well-known examples of such funds are Soros Fund Management and Ziff Brothers Investments, in which all assets under management belong to the partners in the firm or to the head of the firm himself/herself.

So how does one access information on funds?

The **SEC 13-F** filing—a quarterly filing of equity holdings by institutional investment managers having public equity assets under management of $100 million or more—can be used to obtain a fund's long and equity options positions. Note, however, that 13-F filings state only owned assets and long equity positions; short positions are not detailed, as short positions are borrowed, not owned, assets.

Hedge funds that own 5% or more of a particular firm's equity will report these holdings on a **13-D** filing or the abbreviated **13-G** filing essentially meant for passive investors or those who acquired securities "not with the purpose nor with the effect of changing or influencing the control of the "issuer." Hedge funds typically file 13-Gs.

In addition to 13-F, 13-D, and 13-G filings, the SEC Form **ADV** (Part I) has been available on the SEC Web site since February 2006. The ADV Form is the official application for investment advisor registration, and Part I discloses information about the advisor, including assets under management, officers, directors, direct and indirect owners, as well as affiliated funds and advisors and advisors' disciplinary (risk management) history. Note that a number of funds are already registered as investment advisers and their filings can currently be viewed.

The Form ADV Part II is the company's disclosure statement provided to firm clients and is not available to the public.

Online Resources   **Table 6**

Firm Name	Web Site
Albourne Village	www.albournevillage.com
Alternative Investment News	www.iialternatives.com
CSFB/Tremont Hedge Fund Index	www.hedgeindex.com
Hedge Fund Alert	www.hedgefundalert.com
The Hedge Fund Association	www.thehfa.org
HedgeFund.Net *(for accredited investors)*	www.hedgefund.net
Hedge Fund News	www.hedgefundnews.com
Hedge Fund Research	www.hfr.com
Hedge World	www.hedgeworld.com
Managed Account Reports	www.marhedge.com
Managed Funds Association	www.mfainfo.org
Opal Group	www.opalesque.com

There are also several reliable online resources that provide insight on firm news and developments **(Table 6)**. Although funds typically do not have web sites, one can conduct successful searches on the Web by knowing the name of the firm, the fund(s)—often different from the firm name—

Established Hedge Funds/Firms by Selected Strategy[1]

Traditional Long/Short Strategy/Focus

Alson Capital
Andor Capital Management
Ardsley
Basswood Partners
Baupost Group
Blue Ridge Capital
Brandywine Asset Management
Carlson Capital (M)[2]
Chieftain Capital Management
Cumberland Associates
DB Zwirn
Duquesne Capital Management
Farallon Capital Management (M)
Galleon Management
Greenlight Capital (M)
Highbridge Capital (M)
Highfields Capital (A)[3]
Ivory Capital Group
JL Advisors
Knott Partners
Lone Pine Capital
Maverick Capital (M)
Omega Advisors
Pequot Capital Management
Perry Corp. (M)
Renaissance Capital
Royal Capital
SAB Capital (M)
SAC Capital Advisors (M)
Standard Pacific Capital
Third Point Management (A)
Viking Capital
Whitney & Co.
Ziff Brothers Investments

Equity Market Neutral Strategy/Focus (Statistical/Volatility Arbitrage)

AQR Capital Management
Blackthorn Investment Group
Deephaven Capital Management (M)
DE Shaw
Elm Ridge Capital
Fletcher Asset Management
George Weiss Associates
JD Capital
Millenium (M)
Numeric Investors
Paloma Partners
SSI Investment Management
Thales
Tiedemann Investment Group

Distressed Debt Strategy/Focus

Angelo, Gordon & Co.
Appaloosa Management
Avenue Capital
Baupost Group
Canyon Capital Advisors (M)
Cerbeus Capital
Davison Kempner Partners (M)
Elliott Advisors
Farallon Capital Management (M)
Fir Tree Partners
Golden Tree Asset Management
Greenlight Capital (M)
King Street Capital
Longacre Management
MatlinPatterson
Mellon
MHR Management
MW Post Advisory Group
Oaktree Capital
SAB Capital (M)
Satellite Asset Management
Scoggin Capital Management

Global Macro Strategy/Focus

Brevan Howard Asset Management
Bridgewater Associates (M)
Caxton Associates (M)
GAMut Investments Inc
Graham Capital Management
Moore Capital Management (M)
Permal Europe Ltd (Euro)
Quantitative Financial Strategies
Renaissance Technologies
RG Neiderhoffer Capital Management
RHG Capital
Rubicon Fund Management
Soros Fund Management
Tewksbury Capital
Tudor Investment (M)
UBS
Vega Asset Management

Short Selling Strategy/Focus

David W. Tice & Associates
Copper River Management (formerly Rock Partners)
Kynikos Accociates

FOOTNOTES:

1) Established = 5+ year track record and strategy
   capital allocation>=$300 million
2) M= Multistrategy
3) A= Shareholder Activists

Special Situations Strategy/Focus

Amaranth Advisors (M)
American Securities
Angelo, Gordon & Co. (M)
Arnhold and S. Bleichroeder
Atticus Capital
Baker Nye LP
Barep Asset Management
Bitterroot LP
Blackthorn Investment Group
Brencourt Advisors
Cannell Capital (A)
Carlson Capital (M)
Caxton Associates (M)
Chesapeake Partners
Citadel Investment Group (M)
Clinton Group (M)
Davidson Kempner Partners (M)
Deephaven Capital (M)
DKR Capital (M)
Farallon Capital Management (M)
Fir Tree Partners
Gardner Lewis Asset Management
Glenview Capital Management (M)
Gotham Capital
Greenlight Capital (M)
Gruss Asset Management
Halcyon Management
Hamilton Investment Management
Harvest Capital LP
HBK Investments
Highbridge Capital (M)
Highfields Capital
Jay Goldman
Java Partners (A)
John Levin & Co. (M)
K Capital
Kellner, DiLeo & Co.
Kingdon Capital (M)
LibertyView Capital Management
Libra Advisors
Marathon Asset Management (M)
Mariner Investment Group
Mellon
Millenium (M)
Milton Partners
Och-Ziff Capital (M)
Onyx Capital Management
Osprey
Paulson
Perry Corp. (M)
Polygon
Ramius Capital Group
Ritchie Capital Management
SAB Capital (M)
Sagamore Hill Capital Management (M)
Sandell Asset Management (M)
Satellite Asset Management
Scoggin Capital Management
Taconic Capital Advisors
Tiedemann Investment Group
University Capital Strategies Group
Weiss, Peck, and Greer Investments
West Broadway Partners
Westchester Capital
York Capital Management

and fund manager(s).

Other sources of information on particular hedge funds include *Bloomberg News* (Bloomberg terminal needed), which maintains a news section dedicated to hedge funds (type HFND <Go>) and recruiting firms with resources dedicated to hedge fund recruiting **(Section D)**.

As an additional resource on hedge funds, we have included a chart—by no means complete—that segments established firms by firm strategy. We list firms with a 5+ year track record and at least $300 million in assets in a designated strategy. We focus on firms that invest in (1) traditional long/short opportunities, (2) market neutral/arbitrage opportunities, (3) distressed debt opportunities, (4) global macro opportunities, (5) short selling opportunities, and (6) special situations **(Table 7)**. Also, many firms, especially larger ones, are multistrategy **(M)**. We have also identified firms involved in shareholder activism **(A)**, a strategy we explore in greater detail in Section C and which we believe will continue to grow in popularity **(Section C)**.

Below **(Table 8)** we also include a short list of established long-only asset management firms with a fundamental value strategy. These firms are not hedge funds but have been listed nevertheless as they are very well known for their public market style/strategy.

Long-only Asset Management Firms	Table 8
• Baron Capital Group	• Putnam Asset Management
• Capital Research	• Pzena Investment Management
• Davis Advisors	• Royce Asset Management
• Dodge & Cox	• Sequoia
• First Manhattan	• Southeastern
• Harris & Associates	• Sanford Bernstein/Asset Alliance
• Oakmark	• Third Avenue Capital
• Primecap Management	• Wellington Asset Management

FAQ 2 → **What Investment Books Are Recommended?**

All books and reports listed below are on the subject of investing in the public markets and have been recommended by established hedge fund analysts and portfolio managers. Not included--except for Warren Buffet--but equally relevant are the annual letters to shareholders by great business leaders respected by the reader.

We will review in summary detail three books on the list (*), which are conceptual in nature and provide insights into investment thinking. They may help orient those hedge fund candidates just beginning to explore their own investment philosophies and styles.

1	Warren Buffet's Berkshire Hathaway Inc. annual reports
2	Benjamin Graham, *The Intelligent Investor: A Book of Practical Counsel*
3	Joel Greenblatt, *You Can Be a Stock Market Genius**
4	Seth Klarman, *Margin of Safety: Risk-Averse Value Investing Strategies for the Thoughtful Investor*
5	Keith Moore, *Risk Arbitrage: An Investor's Guide*
6	Charles Mullford, Eugene Comiskey, *The Financial Numbers Game: Detecting Creative Accounting Practices*
7	Joseph G. Nicholas, *Investing in Hedge Funds: Strategies for the New Marketplace* and *Market Neutral Investing: Long/Short Hedge Fund Strategies**
8	Jack Schwager, *Market Wizards: Interviews with Top Traders*, and *Stock Market Wizards: Interviews with America's Top Stock Traders*
9	G. Bennett Stewart, III, *The Quest For Value: A Guide for Senior Managers*
10	Nassim Nicholas Taleb, *Fooled by Randomness: The Hidden Role of Chance in the Markets and in Life**

You Can Be a Stock Market Genius by Joseph Greenblatt is a book devoted to "special situations" investing, which includes spin-offs, rights offerings, risk arbitrage, bankruptcy and restructuring, recapitalizations, and stub stocks. Greenblatt, one of the proven masters of special situations investing, writes in a light, fun style and uses examples based on everyday life. By observing regular people's shopping and collecting habits, for instance, he provides an interesting mirror showing how these people might think about investing.

The book begins with "A Few Basics."

The first three points—Do your own work, Don't trust anyone over thirty, and Don't trust anyone thirty or under—are about becoming an independent thinker and not following the lead of others. The latter two points—Pick your spots and Look down, not up—are simply put but challenge some of the most salient points of investment analysis taught in academia and at traditional asset management firms.

- **Do your own work**
- **Don't trust anyone over thirty**
- **Don't trust anyone thirty or under**
- **Pick your spots**
- **Look down, not up**

Greenblatt suggests that an investor pick his spots. He states that the penalty for having a focused portfolio—a slight increase in potential volatility—should be far outweighed by an incremental long-term return. He, along with most hedge fund managers, does not believe in the efficient market or "random-walk" theory that it is not possible to beat the market consistently other than by luck. Clearly, if a candidate were to walk into a hedge fund interview and proclaim—in line with many finance courses—a strong belief in the "random walk" or efficient market theory, he/she would have a lot of explaining to do.

Greenblatt then recommends that "we look down instead of up." He states that risk should be defined by risk of loss, or how much one stands to lose, rather than simply by volatility. He challenges the way the financial community and academia view the concept of risk as applied to the market. Risk, as measured in finance by Beta, or the price volatility of a particular stock relative to the market as a whole, is simplistic and naïve, according to Greenblatt. He provides an example of why: Is a stock that moves significantly over the course of a year really riskier than a stock that moves down slightly during the same period? What if the downside risk on the former stock has been eliminated?

Perhaps Greenblatt's most insightful remarks to a candidate beginning to shape his/her own investment style come when he follows the shopping habits of antique and art collectors, viewing them as investors. There are those who look for undiscovered works of art or antiques priced far below fair value. These shoppers scout country auctions, antique stores, and estate sales, asking whether comparable pieces of furniture or paintings have recently sold at prices far above the potential purchase price.

Alternatively, there are those who ask: "Is this painter going to be the next Picasso?" or "Is eighteenth-century French furniture going to skyrocket in value?" These collectors are trying to predict a trend. In a nutshell, there are those who enjoy studying the present, and then there are those who enjoy trying to predict the future, an interesting but very difficult endeavor.

In both cases, enjoyment must be a part of the process. In a final chapter titled "All the Fun's in Getting There," Greenblatt reminds us that to be a successful investor over the long term, "you must also pretty much enjoy the journey." There are those who inherently enjoy investing and discovering undervalued and overvalued assets and those who do not.

Market Neutral Investing: Long/Short Hedge Fund Strategies by Joseph G. Nicholas defines "market neutral investing" as an approach that seeks to limit exposure to market or systemic—as opposed to company-specific—changes in price caused by shifts in macroeconomic variables or market sentiment. For example, a macroeconomic variable such as interest rate changes can systematically affect the stock prices of an entire industry or sector in a certain direction, while a company's failed product launch will affect a particular company only. Such strategies are open only to the risks associated with what Nicholas calls relationship investing in which performance comes from the net result of the long and short components in a portfolio.

As Nicholas explains, market neutral strategies trade exposure to the markets for exposure to the relationship between the long and short sides of a portfolio. In many cases the short component hedges, or neutralizes, part of the long exposure, leaving an unhedged, residual, directional exposure. Market neutral approaches do not eliminate risk entirely; rather they are meant to allow managers to hedge unwanted market risks and retain exposure to risks they wish to maintain.

Nicholas goes on to explore the following market neutral strategies in considerable detail: convertible arbitrage, merger arbitrage, fixed-income arbitrage, mortgage-backed securities arbitrage, equity market neutral, statistical arbitrage, relative value arbitrage, and equity hedge.

Before leaving the subject of neutrality, we should leave you with a remark a senior volatility arbitrageur once made when asked about market neutral strategies: "There's no such thing as neutrality."

Nassim Nicholas Taleb's book, *Fooled by Randomness: The Hidden Role of Chance in the Markets and in Life*, is written in an easy manner using fun, illustrative examples. Taleb combines philosophy, natural sciences, statistics, literature, and derivatives trading in order to tackle issues in risk, probability, and, as the title suggests, the nature of randomness. Taleb refers to himself as a "crisis hunter" who buys "out-of-the-money" options ("out-of-the-money" options are defined as options that would lead to a negative cash flow if exercised immediately) as he tries to benefit from random events that do not tend to repeat themselves frequently but present a large payoff when they do occur. As a result of his investment style, Taleb claims that he loses money frequently but in small amounts and makes money rarely but in large amounts.

In one of his chapters, Taleb reminds the reader that over a short time horizon, one mostly observes the variability, and not the returns, of a portfolio: "I always remind myself that what one observes is at best a combination of variance and returns, not just returns." He then lists some of the key foibles of traders:

- **AN OVERESTIMATION OF THE ACCURACY OF THEIR BELIEFS IN SOME MEASURE, EITHER ECONOMIC OR STATISTICAL**
- **A TENDENCY TO GET MARRIED TO POSITIONS**
- **A TENDENCY TO CHANGE THEIR STORY**
- **NO PRECISE GAME PLAN AHEAD OF TIME AS TO WHAT TO DO IN THE EVENT OF LOSS**
- **THE ABSENCE OF CRITICAL THINKING, EXPRESSED IN THE ABSENCE OF REVISION OF THEIR STANCE WITH "STOP LOSSES"**
- **DENIAL**

And for candidates who might be proud of their investment track record or who might discuss their track record when prompted, as is often the case in an interview, Taleb's stories are a good reminder to be wary of track records.

Taleb provides the example of a mysterious letter: You get an anonymous letter on January 2 informing you that the stock market will rise during the month of January. You ignore the letter, but it turns out to be true. You receive another letter on February 1 that states the market will go down. Again, it proves to be true. You get a letter on March 1—same story. By

July you are intrigued, and you decide to invest, based on the letter's recommendation. You pour a large part of your savings into the market, and two months later you lose everything. What happened?

The con artist who sends these letters pulls 10,000 names out of a phone book. He mails a bullish letter to half and a bearish letter to half. Next month he mails only to the half (5,000) who received the correct prediction and does the same thing (2,500) the following month. The list soon narrows to 500. You were one of those "lucky" 500.

Taleb then turns to a more apropos example, using 10,000 fictional investment managers, assuming each has a 50 percent probability of making $10,000 at year end and a 50 percent probability of losing $10,000. At the end of the first year, 5,000 are up; after the second year, 2,500 are up; and when another year goes by, 1,250 are up. In the fourth year, 625 are up and in the fifth year, 313 money managers have made money five years straight, out of pure luck! Next he takes the bad ones (one down year) and lets them continue, now with a 45 percent probability of ending up and a 55 percent probability of ending down. In the fifth year, there are 184 winners!

In conclusion, randomness matters. And size matters: The number of managers with great track records depends far more on the number of people who started investing (versus going to dental school, for example) rather than on their ability to produce profits. There would be more excellent managers five years out if they had had a bigger entry class.

C

INTERVIEWS

Who Gets to the First Round?

Before elaborating on how analysts and traders get to and through the interviewing process, two key points should be made from the start. First, most hedge funds are still small in terms of number of employees and back-office infrastructure. Therefore, with the exception of only the largest hedge funds, a portfolio manager or senior analyst or senior trader, as opposed to a human resources person, will typically review a resume directly when deciding to invite someone for an interview.

Second, an interviewer is looking for a cultural/personality fit. Generally sought-after personal characteristics include the following:

- **Innate interest in investing/trading and/or strong ability to analyze drivers of business value**
- **Relentless drive for getting facts, details**
- **Humbleness, capable of admitting a mistake**
- **Hunger to succeed and excel**
- **Work hard/work smart combination**
- **Someone who will stay for the long term, through good times and tough times**

The PM usually looks for a compatible investment or trading fit as well. In some firms, however, and especially for more junior hires, a fully developed or shared style is not as important as the above mentioned character traits and an openness to learn and to be molded.

Those candidates who understand that the hedge fund recruiting process is a two-way matching process and have therefore spent time making sure their investment style and interests and/or character traits match those of the firm are much more likely to advance to second and third rounds. What one often finds is that candidates have spent relatively too much time preparing investment ideas and relatively too little time studying the person and the firm to whom they will be presenting their ideas. No matter how brilliant an idea, if you are pitching a momentum-driven technical short-term trade to a long-term investor who focuses on fundamental drivers of equity value, you are wasting your time and theirs.

Meanwhile it's always wise to think about what is going through the mind of the interviewer: Rest assured that the interviewer is usually thinking whether he/she would want to keep the

Interviews

prospective employee at the firm long term; at hedge funds there is no two-year program, after which time you are encouraged to get an MBA or find something else to do, as with banking and consulting programs. He/she is also carefully considering the asymmetric cost of your potential compensation versus the relatively huge amount of capital the firm stands to lose through poor investment or trading judgment.

ANALYSTS

Preferred for analyst positions are those candidates with some public equity asset management experience on the long and/or short side and a demonstrated interest in the profession of investing. Those with private-equity experience and a demonstrable interest in public sector investing are usually next in line, followed by sell-side research analysts and then investment bankers and consultants working in finance-focused consulting practices (*alternative investment news*, January 2003). Others who may be considered have industry-specific experience that is relevant to a particular hedge fund or have a credible story on how particular skills sets learned through other work experiences—investigative reporting skills or doctoral-level research skills, for example—are transferable to hedge fund analyst positions. For the more junior level positions (junior analyst), the playing field is more even, as less work experience is required.

In general, there are two types of PMs who consider hiring analysts with little to no public market investing experience. There are those who seek candidates with a "passion" for the markets, those who are truly interested in and enjoy investing. Typically such candidates regularly read *Barron's*, *The Wall Street Journal*, and other financial news or wire services and think about particular stocks thoroughly. These candidates are interested in digging into 10-Ks and 10-Qs, they have a well-developed point of view and detailed information on several stocks at any given time, they follow corporate earnings announcements/conference calls, and they are ready to discuss their ideas on short notice in a way that exhibits depth of knowledge and consistency in analytical thought. Such candidates are akin, by analogy, to the kid who read every car magazine well before he could afford his own car, studying and comparing every detail of every part, manufacturer, model, and price tag.

Then there are those PMs who look for candidates with an "interest" in as opposed to a "passion" for the markets and who have a very specific skill set or industry expertise. These candidates typically have strong aptitudes for independent thinking and analysis of drivers of business value and are good with brainteasers or general case studies with financial implications.

There are also two types of analyst positions—the industry generalist position and the sector or industry specialist position. For the PM who seeks a generalist, specific skill sets can include financial modeling and business analysis. For the PM seeking industry expertise, industry experience and financial analysis will be tested. In both cases, however, ambition, drive, and cultural fit are essential. The ability to learn, a high level of curiosity, and open-mindedness are also sought-after personality characteristics.

TRADERS

Generally sought-after trader characteristics include the following:

- **Poor, Smart, with a Desire to become rich ("PSD"), term coined by Bear Stearn's Ace Greenberg; alternatively Poor, Hungry, Determined ("PHD")**
- **Energetic, tenacious**
- **Proactive, aggressive, "pitbulls"**

Buy-side and sell-side execution traders perform similar functional roles on a day-to-day basis. However, many portfolio managers state that for experienced hires the transition from sell-side execution to buy-side execution is not always straightforward. The buy-side execution trader has more of a focus on execution optimization, whereas sell-side execution traders may be more client-service oriented and may pursue market share strategies at the cost of the firm's P&L. In addition, the information flow on the sell-side is much greater than on the buy-side, forcing the hedge fund buy-side trader to conduct market trading due diligence proactively. A buy-side trader is also expected to understand the nature of risk management and portfolio management associated with the strategy employed by his/her fund. Some PMs have remarked on the "trades beget trades" phenomenon apparent among some sell-side traders trying to manage risk.

For junior traders, personality fit cannot be overestimated in the interviewing process. Says one PM on interviewing junior traders: "I think it's hard to prepare because the qualities traders are looking for are very much personality traits." Personality traits typically include a team-player outlook, a penchant for numbers, and an exhibited ability to grow into a value-added resource beyond some of the relatively routine trading functions.

FAQ 4 → **Who Gets Past the First Round?**

A candidate who holds a substantiated and consistent point of view on investment or trading ideas and has a specific skill set relevant to the position being sought stands a strong chance of making it past round one, assuming he/she exhibits the aforementioned personal characteristics.

Once again, there are two types of PMs, those who seek the "passionate" investor and those who seek the "interested" investor who has a particular skill set or intellectual aptitude. Note that in the former case, when it comes to an investing or trading idea, a PM wants to hear about what to invest in today or tomorrow, not an idea that would have been good yesterday or six months ago. Those firms that seek a passionate investor or someone whose interest level shines above his/her peers will most likely ask some of the following questions:

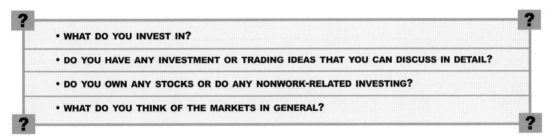

- **WHAT DO YOU INVEST IN?**
- **DO YOU HAVE ANY INVESTMENT OR TRADING IDEAS THAT YOU CAN DISCUSS IN DETAIL?**
- **DO YOU OWN ANY STOCKS OR DO ANY NONWORK-RELATED INVESTING?**
- **WHAT DO YOU THINK OF THE MARKETS IN GENERAL?**

Those who make it past the first round do not have stale answers to these questions. Fresh investment ideas, in a manner consistent with the firm's investment style, are essential. And those who actively think about trading or investing typically move to the next round.

Hedge funds conduct three or four rounds of interviews before hiring a candidate. The second round can be more of an on-the-spot investment or trading case study. The candidate will meet more members of the firm to reinforce the perception that there is both a good cultural and, in most cases, investment-style fit.

In theory, if there's time for a full-blown third round, the firm might ask the candidate to pitch another idea, either in person or in the format of a take-home case study. For highly quantitative-driven strategies there will be further exploration of a specific skill set. By the fourth round, the fund managers or traders will have met and have decided to move forward with an offer, assuming the fourth round goes well.

Who Does Not Get to the First Round?

Candidates who exhibit a pure "sell-side" or client-driven mentality—in contrast to a buy-side or principle-side mentality—will generally not get to or past the first-round interview. Candidates who highlight the volume of transactions or engagements they've completed in banking or trading are a red flag to many PMs. Sell-side bankers are often rewarded for their ability to initiate, process, and close deals. But PMs are more interested in thought processes and risk management than in the deal or flow volume. In addition, most PMs who practice the fundamentals of rigorous value investing are more interested in a well thought through point of view than the sort of broad sensitivity analyses in sell-side financial models that give analysts significant "wiggle room" in coming up with a specific valuation.

We will revisit this topic in our discussion of resumes **(Section E)**, where we will also address candidates who tend to exaggerate their love of investing by writing strong statements in the personal section of their resumes. Doing so is a great way to get tangled up early on if there is little backup to support such claims.

Finally, candidates who want to leave their current situations because prospects are not what they once were or primarily for compensation reasons or those who seem unfocused in their job search and are open to "anything on the buy-side" (private equity, hedge funds, etc.) will not fare well relative to those who are driven to a hedge fund for the opportunity to invest or trade in public equities.

Professionals and candidates with strong pedigrees—be it in schooling and/or professional experience—should be mindful that entering a hedge fund is like starting from scratch. The first year is an apprenticeship. Any sense of entitlement communicated in a resume or e-mail to a PM or recruiting professional on such topics as guaranteed compensation or a clearly delineated career track at a hedge fund will not be well received.

For the most part hedge funds are meritocratic. An individual's performance, investment style or trading habits, and acquired skill sets are critical, whereas postcollege pedigrees, in general, are relatively insignificant—except to the extent that such postcollege pedigreed candidates tend to be highly motivated, driven, and intelligent. All these characteristics are necessary but not always sufficient for many of the opportunities at hedge funds.

RED FLAGS

Getting to Round 1:

resume, correspondence, initial screening

- "Sell-side"/ client-driven mentality

- Lack of focus in job search

- Deal focused/ volume focused

- Exaggerated love of investing (see Resume, Section E)

- Grass is greener mentality

- Entitlement

- Investment fit

Finally those who have not exhibited ambition, drive, and a cultural fit with a particular fund will not make it to the first round. This lack of fit will come out, in some way, in a resume or e-mail to a PM or recruiter.

Who Does Not Get Past the First Round?

*T*he first round is often like dating, says one PM. *"You may not know if the person across the table is right for you, but on the first date you will know if there's not a chance at all."*

Those who discuss their inability to invest or think about investment ideas—due to time constraints or current employer restrictions on trading—do not make it past the first round. There are too many candidates with similar such restrictions who find the time to think about investment ideas and who trade and track fictional or, "paper," portfolios. Nor does a candidate who speaks about investing in stock ideas interesting a year ago or brilliant from hindsight or that are more appropriate to a 401-K plan or pension plan than to a fund that typically looks for interesting, undiscovered, undervalued, or overvalued equities. And as mentioned earlier, a treatise on the beauty of the efficient market or "random walk" theory will get little respect from most hedge fund managers.

In general, candidates often dig their own graves when interviewing by pronouncing a strong interest in or passion for the markets or trading without being able to substantiate it with consistent logic or deep thought. Others discuss how well they have performed in their personal account (PA) as opposed to how they think about investing. An interviewer is looking for talent with consistency of thought and a person who can withstand the market in both good and bad times. They are looking for someone whose commitment to their fund is long term. So as a note to the young, entrepreneurial investor: It may not be wise to blurt out a desire to work a few years before starting your own fund. This may be true, but it can be disconcerting to a PM who is looking for a long-term prospect. As a reminder, most hedge funds do not expect an analyst to leave after two years for his/her MBA or to start his own fund. Portfolio managers generally view new hires as apprentices and are looking for candidates who understand what an apprenticeship means and are not looking for neatly delineated career steps, titles, and guarantees or a career launching pad for something else or grander plans elsewhere.

RED FLAGS

Round 1:

Interview

- **No time to invest**

- **Unable to invest due to current company restrictions**

- **Stale investment ideas, noncurrent investment ideas**

- **Random Walk missionaries**

- **Careerists focused on job titles, promotions, guarantees**

- **Personal Accounts success stories**

- **Pure entrepreneurs**

- **Inconsistencies in asset class preference, investment style, investing holding periods**

- **Inconsistencies between stated investment strategy/style and investment decisions made in Personal Account (PA)**

For funds that seek a candidate with a particular style or strategy, a quiet interviewer simply needs to listen for 30 minutes to a candidate speak about investing to determine if he/she is consistent in his/her approach to investing.

In general, consistency of thought throughout the interviewing process is critical, as opposed to opportunistic thinking or investing strategies that could make a PM worried about opportunistic "style-shift." Particular inconsistencies that interviewers are on the lookout for include those that show shifts throughout the conversation in one's stated preference for asset class, investment style, and investing holding periods.

Interview Questions

The analyst interview questions or format is predicated to some degree on whether the firm wants to hire a generalist or an industry specialist and whether the firm tends to hire those with a passion for investing versus an interest in investing in the public markets.

Firms that seek an industry generalist with an interest in market investing will typically assess a candidate's raw intelligence or specific financial skill sets by giving brainteasers or case studies laced with finance underpinnings. For example, a case study may ask about the risks and rewards associated with investing in a precious metals company versus investing in a firm that processes a commodity such as timber or coal.

Firms that seek a specialist will focus almost exclusively on depth of industry knowledge and whether the candidate's knowledge base and investment style would benefit the firm. Firms that seek passion will tend to let the candidate speak about his/her own ideas, always testing for freshness of ideas and rigor and consistency of analytical thought.

A fund's strategy may also drive the type of questions a candidate will be asked. Questions often reflect what the PMs do on a typical day and the sorts of decisions they have to make.

Whether a firm seeks an industry generalist or a specialist, whether it is looking to hire a passionate investor or one with a strong interest in the markets, whether it seeks someone for a specific strategy, all managers are looking for someone who can seek out and size and profit from value discrepancies in the marketplace while understanding the underlying risks associated with their investment decisions.

A PM at a fundamental value fund that is not event driven or catalyst driven can typically do this in one of two ways. They can either ask general high-level questions about investing or company-specific questions. As a general question, a manager might ask what you would invest in if you could invest in anything, anywhere in the world, and why. The question, general as it may sound, tests a candidate's ability to think creatively about asset classes, including but not limited to equity, debt, currencies, and commodities and also tests a candidate's ability to value, size, and profit from the opportunity and the risks associated with such an opportunity.

INTERVIEW QUESTION

If you could invest in anything, anywhere in the world, what would it be, and why?

When a PM asks about a company-specific scenario, the discussion will focus on a company's operating fundamentals and financial valuation. Value fund managers will expect a candidate to incorporate relevant public, private, and takeover multiples as well as all key operational assumptions driving business value in his/her formation of an equity valuation. A value fund with an analytical focus on discounted cash flow valuation (DCF) and intrinsic value may, for instance, focus on such issues as terminal values, discount rates, and growth rates and expect a candidate to discuss how his/her DCF model might differ from or improve on a sell-side DCF model. Areas for improvement include a thoroughly thought through point of view on the equity risk premium, forward-looking operating margins and growth rates, and the most appropriate inputs for the terminal value. A candidate will be given a company to analyze or if the PM seeks a passionate investor, will be expected to generate all investment ideas discussed.

As candidates prepare for interviews at such fundamental value funds, it is useful for them to review frameworks that get to the drivers of business value and focus on the most relevant financial and operational metrics. One such framework, which has received widespread recognition and acceptance, was pioneered in 1919 by The Du Pont Company and is worth reviewing.

THE DUPONT SYSTEM OF ANALYSIS: ASSESSING THE EFFICIENCY AND VALUE OF A FIRM

The DuPont System Expresses the Return on Assets as:

ROA = Operating Profit Margin Ratio * Asset Turnover Ratio

where Operating Profit Margin Ratio = Net Income from Operations + Interest Expense/Gross Revenue

where Asset Turnover = Gross Rev/Avg Assets

The DuPont System Expresses the Return on Equity as:

ROE = (ROA - Interest Expense/Average Assets) * Equity Multiplier

where Equity Multiplier = (Avg Assets/Avg Equity)

The DuPont System of Analysis, originally used to determine the strengths and weaknesses of a farm, merges the income statement and balance sheet into two summary measures of profitability: Return on Assets (ROA) and Return on Equity (ROE). The system uses three financial ratios to tell us that ROE is affected by three things: the Operating Profit Margin Ratio (OPM), which measures operating efficiency, the Asset Turnover Ratio (ATR), which measures asset use efficiency, and the Equity Multiplier (EM), which measures financial leverage and efficiency.

Any decision affecting the product prices, per unit costs, volume or efficiency has an impact on the profit margin or turnover ratios. Similarly any decision affecting the amount and ratio of debt or equity used will affect the financial structure and the overall cost of capital of a company. Understanding the interrelationships among the various ratios such as turnover ratios, leverage, and profitability ratios helps focus a candidate's valuation of a particular company.

Special situations/event driven investing involves making investments in specific catalyst-driven scenarios unfolding in the marketplace; these scenarios include such "extraordinary" (outside the normal business cycle) corporate events as spin-offs, rights offerings, risk/merger arbitrage, bankruptcy and restructuring, recapitalizations, and stub stocks. They also include less extraordinary but no less important catalysts such as regulatory issues, new product introductions, and management changes.

A **special situations/event driven** PM focused on *merger arbitrage* will typically ask for a candidate's point of view on a proposed merger deal or an announced spin-off currently unfolding in the news. The PM would expect the candidate to know what deals are unfolding and ask him/her to pick one and discuss.

A candidate should also be very familiar with the various valuation methodologies used in mergers and acquisitions analyses and the different types of deal structures, for instance, whether it is a cash and/or equity deal, whether the acquirer is a public or a private entity, and whether the acquiree is public or private.

In addition, the candidate should have thought through some of the key issues a risk arbitrageur faces when a deal is announced, for example, the role of regulatory agencies in the merger/arbitrage process of an announced deal. Ultimately the arbitrageur is expected to know how to find mispricings that allow him/her to make money. (See Keith Moore's book recommendation in the

"Hedge Funds" section).

In speaking with successful and experienced risk arbitrageurs who have lived through various risk arbitrage cycles, a few general themes emerge. First, the biggest change over time has been the enormous information flow now available and the ease of accessing such data--as one well-known practitioner put it, "we've gone from a one-shoot deck to a six-shoot deck," and from a time when "have to go downtown to manually pick up the (10)Ks and (10)Qs" to a time when all information is Web accessible. Second, each cycle has been different. Third, and perhaps most important, though the risk/merger arbitrage process used to be the primary part of any serious analysis in determining whether a transaction would be completed, now credit skills and equity valuation skills are equally important. So is knowing the fundamentals of the firm and all the players involved in the deal, "right down to the legal teams behind the deal," according to a business veteran.

Finally in thinking through both how to profit from value discrepancies as well as how to size up the discrepancies, note that merger arbitrage situations can provide attractive annualized risk adjusted rewards but may provide little absolute return. Earning 5 cents on a $2 stock in a month may provide an attractive annualized return of 30% but only so long as it can be repeated each month. A company merger/acquisition is typically a discrete one-time event in any given year.

A PM at a **special situations/event-driven** fund that focuses on *distressed and/or bankruptcy* investing will ask about a distressed situation currently unfolding as well. A PM would expect the candidate to be aware of those sections and exhibits of the 10-K, 10-Q, and 8-K (Report of Unscheduled Material Events) wherein are contained credit agreements, amendments to credit agreements, and bond indentures. Other key sources a candidate would be expected to know are Moody's and S&P reports/credit ratings, and, in the case of bankruptcies, the bankruptcy documents available on bankruptcy court Web sites.

A **capital structure/event-driven** PM would want a candidate to be well versed in the quantitative models and theories (Example: Merton model) relevant to this particular strategy and to incorporate into a discussion the relevant SEC filings in an informed convertible arbitrage trading position. These filings include the firm prospectus, S-3, and S-4 filings. A PM could ask about a convertible arbitrage trade within a firm's debt structure or across the capital structure (debt/equity).

CANNELL CAPITAL LLC

June 1, 2005

BKF Capital Group, Inc.
One Rockefeller Plaza, 25th Floor
New York, NY 10020

"When, O Catiline, do you mean to cease abusing our patience? How long is that madness of yours still to mock us? When is there to be an end of that unbridled audacity of yours, swaggering about as it does now?"

Thus, in 63 B.C., did Marcus Tullius Cicero expose corruption and vice in theRoman Senate in his First Oration Against Lucius Catilina. His words are relevant today as we study the record of BKF Capital Group.

Fund management should be a challenging yet simple business -- control costs, manage investments intelligently, and fees will flow to the bottom line. Revenues from incremental assets should require little additional expense.

But that is not BKF. Costs are exorbitant. A culture of greed and self-dealing has run amok. Incremental revenues are sucked up by inflated salaries; as a result, BKF continues to lose money, even as assets and revenues have grown 18% and 64%, respectively, over the last five years. Management has frittered away its gains in revenues, producing greater losses, while distributing, at shareholder expense, a staggering 78% of revenues to the executive cabal. Meanwhile, the Board of Directors, whose job it should be to protect the rights of shareholders, and not protect entrenched management, has failed to discharge its fiduciary duties by reigning in run-away compensation and other costs...

...BKF's richly-compensated employees, egregious occupancy costs and ill-defined "other operating expenses" are not in the best interest of shareholders. BKF's operating metrics (operating margin, revenue-per-employee, etc.) are abysmal.

Comparisons to similar publicly-traded companies reveal the mismanagement.

$MM	Company	AUM	Revenues	Op. Margin	Employees	Revenue/ Employee	Cost/ Employee
CLMS	Calamos	$38,000	$342.8	45%	264	$1,298.5	$248.9
GBL	Gabelli	28,700	255.2	39%	188	1,357.4	553.7
HNNA	Hennessy Advisors	1,261	9.5	50%	10	954.5	201.6
TROW	T. Rowe Price	45,200	1,277.0	41%	4,139	308.5	110.6
LIO LN	Liontrust	5,035	24.5	35%	43	569.4	369.3
BKF	BKF Capital	$13,604	$126.5	4%	151	$837.7	$634.1

Source: Factset, 2004 SEC 10-Ks

BKF's April 22, 2005 Form 8-K discloses the compensation arrangements for the managers of the event-driven portfolios, Messrs. Frank Rango and Henry Levin (the son of BKF's Chairman & CEO). The Board's passivity allows the Managers to pay their team up to 67% of the event-driven group's revenue. The Managers are entitled to a base salary of $800,000 and are incentivized with 67% of the group's remaining net profit. The gravy train doesn't end there, however. If BKF terminates Rango and Levin without cause, each will enjoy severance payments of between $2 million and $4 million. There are no restrictions on their ability to solicit BKF's investors or employees if they leave. None of the Managers' compensation is in the form of BKF equity. None of their compensation is in the form of long-term incentives, which would encourage retention. How are these arrangements supposed to align the interests of the Managers with the well-being of your stockholders? All this excess would be dandy in a private company, but BKF is public...

...BKF's list of "related party transactions" reads like comic monkeyshines. If the compensation committee must bless paying 78% of the Company's earnings to Mr. Levin, his relatives and intimates, at least pay them in stock. This would align the interests of the business operators with the business owners. It would also provide employees greater after-tax benefits. I suspect most BKF employees labor under the oppressive yoke of federal, state, and New York City income and sales taxes. Long-term capital gains rates of 15% on stock-based compensation would offer them far greater economic benefit. Please us by pleasing them.

The callous conflagration of shareholder assets by BKF galls us as it would gall Cicero. When we visit companies, we stay at $39.95 motels, not fancy hotels with fruit at the "reception" desk. If the bathroom glasses are not wrapped in paper, we flee. We are not squired about in Lincoln Town cars driven by perfumed menservants (although admittedly, Cannell Capital LLC squandered $1,200 on The Donkey Van, http://donkeynation.com, a used 1995 Ford Econoline van, purchased from See's Candies, Inc. in 2004).

My visit to your offices on May 26, 2005 left me astounded that such an unprofitable company would house itself in some of the most expensive office space in America. Your 56,000 square foot office in Rockefeller Center immolates cash at the expense of BKF's shareholders. Why dedicate half a floor to "test" Dell computers? Not all meretricious trappings are poor business expenses, however. I appreciate the lavish spending of casinos as they lure "whales" to their tables, but this acceptance is predicated upon such adornments being accretive to earnings, to bringing in profitable bacon. Your Rockefeller Center pork just stinks...

...One would expect such deportment from scalawags, but not you noble nabobs of Wall Street. I hoped for better from Mr. Biggs, who built an illustrious career offering advice to investors -- which BKF so plainly needs. I hoped for better from Professor Malkiel, who has directed Vanguard Group as a paragon of financial probity and responsibility. I hoped for better from Mr. Beard. It's hard to believe that this is the same Beard who, in a May 12, 2005 letter to Morgan Stanley shareholders wrote:

> *"Shareholders deserve better. We strongly believe that new leadership is critical to the success of the Firm and to the creation of shareholder value."*

The boards' lack of credible hedge fund experience is a hindrance to BKF. Though burnished, bespoke and credentialed, I see little in the directors, save James Tisch, which suggests any operating experience in its quiver. I am not interested in managing BKF or any of its assets. (In fact, Cannell Capital has distributed over $250 million back to investors in recent years in order to remain nimble.) But BKF's board should include people with credible hedge fund management expertise and long term track records. BKF has grown since the November 1995 merger of Baker Fentress with John A. Levin & Co., but in the last five years, BKF has generated $464.6 million in revenues, but no profits. Indeed, BKF has racked up $62.4 million in losses Mr. Levin operates BKF like a private playpen. He does not appear to value stockholders as important partners or constituents.

I therefore urge the Board either to: (i) take BKF private and squander privately; (ii) appoint an investment banker to conduct an auction of the company, as Opportunity Partner's Phillip Goldstein first suggested in his November 17, 2003 13d filing; or (iii) stand down and pass the baton to a shareholder-friendly board.

We today speak with many interested parties who are on deck to increase the efficiency and productivity of your operations, energize the investment team to spark greater performance and substantially increase assets under management. Please consider this latter "dream team" option.

Cicero ultimately vanquished Catiline despite the latter's attempt to form a rebel force with other rich and corrupt men.

> *"The city should rejoice because it has been saved from a bloody rebellion. He asked for nothing for himself but the grateful remembrance of the city for what he has done. He acknowledged that this victory was more difficult than one in foreign lands, because the enemies were citizens of Rome."*

You still have time to flee. Go forth, Catiline.

Sincerely,

J. Carlo Cannell
Managing Member

Another type of event-driven investing involves shareholder activism, which distinguishes itself from other forms of event-driven investing in that the investor is creating the event itself, as opposed to responding to a specific above-mentioned corporate event/special situation. The shareholder activist letter typifies the sort of shareholder activism that attempts to unlock shareholder value by forcing a change in the behavior of a corporation through the influence of the firm's investor base.

An interviewer might ask a candidate to describe a company situation that is ripe for shareholder activism. Since activist investments tend to be fairly concentrated and are often not very liquid, substantial in-depth analysis is usually performed before making such investments. Therefore qualified applicants will often be expected to demonstrate excellent valuation skills in addition to great research skills.

A candidate seeking an analyst role at a **market neutral** fund should be prepared to discuss or show proficiency in quantitative investment theory, stochastic volatility models, multifactor regression models, and/or the application of other linear and nonlinear quantitative models to sector-

Interviews

C

specific public market investing.

A **global macro** PM may want a candidate to discuss the implications of a current event and how it will affect various asset class markets around the world. A PM would expect the candidate to discuss macroeconomic data, be familiar with charting time series and examining leading/lagging relationships between economic indicators, and have the ability to cull and summarize succinctly vast amounts of sell-side research on economic variables across industries and geographies.

Assessment Tools and Personality Tests

A growing number of established hedge funds are using assessment tools as screening devices in the interview process. After the initial rounds of interviews have been successfully passed by candidates, some hedge funds have been utilizing a variety of tests, ranging from personality/IQ tests to knowledge skills and abilities tests. Hedge funds that incorporate such tests in the interviewing process believe they provide some insight into potential behavior and job-related progress and performance that are otherwise difficult to judge in the standard interviewing process.

Personality tests such as the Caliper test may be administered to evaluate a wide variety of "softer qualities" such as individual personality characteristics, motivations, and potential strengths as well as possible limitations. The Caliper is a comprehensive 180-question personality test with sections ranging from mathematical sequences, number series and letter patterns, and verbal analogies to self-assessment questions about whether you "least likely agree" or "most likely agree" with certain statements.

Other assessment tools may also be used, such as the Brainbench skills test, which is usually applicable more for Information Technology (IT) and programming-focused positions. These software simulations are used to test the level and quality of skills and abilities that are crucial for job performance. Brainbench tests can be used to assess the candidates' computer programming/ development skills and capabilities, such as C++, Java, VBA, SQL, Matlab languages, just to name a few. These tests are typically administered for Quantitative Trader, Trader/Developer, and Application Developer type positions at hedge funds.

We estimate that approximately one in five established hedge funds are administering these standardized tests. All things considered, hedge fund managers will rely on their own instincts and judgment in addition to such test scores, except of course for the IT and programming positions for which such test results are of paramount importance.

D

RECRUITERS

Getting the Interview

Despite the hedge fund industry's continued state of growth, with an estimated 8,000 funds and assets under management now estimated at approximately $1.5 trillion—a more than tenfold increase in ten years—the number of jobs available for experienced hires or for students through on-campus recruiting, although growing, is still limited. This distinguishes hedge funds from investment banking and consulting firms, which in periods of growth hire armies of new staff at a time.

Recruiting in the hedge fund industry is fragmented and typically does not follow any official recruiting season, as is typically the case with most financial services and consulting firms. This fragmentation and the nonseasonal factor are both a blessing and a curse: a blessing in that no one MBA program or banking program or private equity firm is a primary feeder into the industry, effectively leveling the playing field for any hungry candidate with passion or a specific skill set for the markets; a curse, as there can be significant legwork involved in securing a hedge fund position.

In regard to the blessing, it is interesting to note that the number of hedge funds that actually recruit at the top-ranked MBA programs and the number of MBA candidates who receive full-time hedge fund job offers are slim but growing. Some of the top MBA programs' marketing collateral have boasted a veritable Who's Who of top-tier hedge fund recruiting partners for years, and yet this list is only now becoming a reality.

About 25-30 funds recruited on campus for full-time positions at top MBA programs in each of the last two years and at least that many posted on the schools' electronic job boards. Approximately 4-6% of the class at leading MBA programs joined hedge funds upon graduation. About 15-20 funds appeared on campus at the top MBA programs in 2003-2004 and at least that many posted on the schools' electronic job boards. No more than 5-10 hedge funds appeared on campus in 2002-2003 when no more than 2% of the class joined hedge funds upon graduation. And one need only go back to the MBA graduating classes of 2001 to note that full-time positions and summer internships at hedge funds barely existed and the rare position was simply categorized under the long-only asset management category of MBA employment data (example: 2001 Stanford Graduate School of Business Employment Report). Most programs still do not differentiate between asset management firms and hedge funds.

In addition, hedge fund summer internships are cropping up with greater regularity for MBA candidates who have completed their first year of business school, as established hedge funds are showing signs of formalizing the campus recruiting process. But the overall numbers are still small, given the size and growth rate of the industry and the demand for hedge fund jobs.

Most professionals and students end up conducting a "self-directed" search using alumni networks, professional and personal networks and associations, and recruiting firms that specialize in the hedge fund sector. To understand the importance of networks, one need only ask a recruiter who his/her largest competitor is. It's typically not another recruiting firm but the hedge fund manager's own personal and professional networks.

When it comes to recruiting firms, of which there are hundreds in the finance industry, most are not relevant for candidates dedicated to finding a hedge fund opportunity. Most of the well-known and established publicly traded recruiting firms have not to date been helpful to candidates seeking hedge fund analyst and trader positions, as these recruiting firms tend to focus on much more senior roles in general and primarily employ a full-retainer-based business model that many hedge funds are unwilling to agree to, insisting instead on smaller retainers or simply a pay-for-success model rather than what they see as a pay-regardless-of-success model.

A hedge fund candidate's employment needs are best met by those firms with a staff dedicated to hedge fund recruiting and with a significant track record of past and recent placements for traders and analysts.

Table 9 is a general list—compiled by *Hedge Fund Alert*—of recruiters who work in the hedge fund arena in some capacity. When contacting recruiting firms, one should spend the time asking recruiters about (1) their hedge fund client base and the functional roles and levels for which they have significant experience making placements, (2) the nature of their relationship with their hedge fund clients, and (3) the nature of their relationship with you, the candidate seeking employment. Not captured on this list are a new crop of recruiters who have left senior human resources roles at major funds, including Citadel and Amaranth, to start their own recruitment firms.

Organization	Firm Location	Specialty
Advantage Financial Search	New York City	Investment and operations
Ajilon Finance	New York City	Operations (finance, accounting)
A-L Associates	New York City	Investment (traders, analysts) and operations
Alpha Search Advisory Partners	New York City	Investment
Broadreach Group	New York City	Investment and operations
Capital Group International	St. Louis	Investment (analysts, portfolio managers)
Catalyst Search Group	Lake Forest (IL)	Operations (technology)
Centennial Partners	Connecticut	Investment and marketing
Coleman & Co.	New York City	Investment and operations (marketing, compliance)
Cornell Global	Connecticut	Investment and operations
Corporate Search Partners	Dallas	Investment (research, trading) and marketing
CPI	New York City	Investment (portfolio managers)
Criqui Brogersen	New York City	Investment (analysts)
Cromwell Partners	New York City	Investment and operations
CV Associates	New York City	
David Barrett Partners	New York City	Investment and operations
David Reed & Associates	Connecticut	Investment (analysts, portfolio managers)
Delfino & Parker	New York City	Investment and operations
DHR International	Chicago	Investment and operations
DM Stone Recruitment	San Francisco	
Dunn & Associates	San Francisco	Operations (mid- to upper-level executives)
Dynamic Associates	New York City	
Execu-Search Group	New York City	Investment and operations
First Associates	Chicago	Investment (traders, analysts)
GF Parish Group	Minnesota	Teams
Global Systems Staffing	New York City	Investment (portfolio managers, technology and quantitative analysts)
Glocap Search	New York City	
Grady Levkov & Co.	New York City	Investment (technology and quantitative analysts
Harris & Associates	Columbus	
HF Solutions	New Jersey	Investment
Higdon Barrett	New York City	Investment and operations
Huffman Associates	Long Island	Investment and operations
Hunter Advisors	New York City	Investment (distressed, event-driven, long/short and deep value)
Innovations PSI	San Francisco	Investment and operations
InSite Search	Westport (CT)	Investment (trading) and operations (tech)
Integrated Management Recruiting	Tempe (AZ)	Investment (capital markets, research, trading) and marketing
International Market Recruiters	New York City	Investment (hedge fund due diligence) and trade support
Isaacson Search Co.	New York City	Investment (quantitative analysts)
J. Nicholas Bogard	Boston	
Jamesback Global Partners	New York City	Investment and investor relations
Jilson Advisors	Connecticut	Investment (oil, natural gas, power, metals)
JSB Partners	New York City	Operations (CEOs, CFOs, CCOs, controllers)
Kohn Associates Legal Search	Quebec	Lawyers
Korn/Ferry International	Chicago	Investment and operations
Long Ridge Partners	New York City	Investment and operations
Marston Mills	Chicago	
Meier Group	Minneapolis	Investment (trading) and operations
Mercury Partners	New York City	Investment (research analysts, traders)
Michael Page International	Boston	Investment (quantitative or sector analysts) and operations (CFOs, COOs, finance, compliance)
Mission Staffing	New York City	Operations (accounting, finance, trading)
MJE-ICS Associates	Park (NJ)	
MUSE Network	N/A	Investment and operations(CEOs, CFOs)
Neal Management	New York City	Operations (Finance, accounting, risk)
Olschwanger Partners	Dallas	Investment (portfolio managers) and operations (senior sales, client services)
Open Systems Technologies	New York City	Operations (financial, information technology)
Options Group	New York City, L.A.	
Oxbridge Group	New York City, L.A.	Investment and operations
Parks Legal Placement	Houston	Legal and compliance
Peak Search	New York City	Risk management
Pinnacle Group International	New York City	
Preston & Co.	Clinton (NJ)	Investment and operations
Prince Goldsmith	New York City	Investment and operations
Quest Organization	New York City	Investment and operations
Response Cos.	New York City	Investment and operations

Table continued on next page

D

Recruiters

Organization	Firm Location	Specialty
Ricks & Ray Partners	New York City	Investment and operations (senior level)
Risk Talent Associates	New York City	Risk and compliance
Rothstein Kass Executive Search	New Jersey	Investments (analysts, traders) and operations (accounting, finance, compliance)
Russell Reynolds	New York City	Investment and operations
S. Diamond Group	Fairfield (CT)	Investment and operations
Schaller Consulting	New York City	Investment
Schwab Enterprise	New York City	Investment and operations
Search One	New York City	Investment
Sextant Partners	New York City	Investment and operations (not back office)
SG Partners	New York City	Investment and operations
Sinon Group	New York City	Investment and operations
Smith Hanley	New York City, Chicago	Investment (trading, risk management, technology)
Smyth Associates	New York City	
Spencer Stuart	New York City	Investment and operations
Steven Douglass & Associates	Weston (FL)	Operations (business development)
Taylor Grey	Connecticut	Operations
Teeman Perley Gilmartin	New York City	Investment and operations
Wall Street Options	New York City	Investment and operations
Warren International	New York City	Teams
Westminster Group	Chester (SC)	Operations (marketing, sales, accounting)

Source: Hedge Fund Alert, January 2006

Some firms primarily conduct front-office searches—which typically include analysts, PMs, and traders—whereas others focus on infrastructure roles. Some work with established hedge funds with sizable assets under management, whereas others focus on hedge fund start-ups. Note that 50% of hedge funds have less than $38 million in assets under management, according to Bernstein Research (*The Hedge Fund Industry: Products, Services or Capabilities?*, June 2003). It is important to determine the size and history of the funds being represented as there are different career issues associated with each. For example, the failure rate of hedge fund start-ups is high, 10%-20% according to industry estimates, and small funds cannot withstand several years of poor performance. As a result, most professionals looking to start a career in hedge funds gravitate to larger, more established funds, even if that means the inability early on to obtain equity in the firm.

Some recruiting firms are very close to their clients; others are not. Some recruiters themselves have significant professional experience in finance and therefore effectively serve as a first round interview/screen for their clients; others simply provide clients with resumes based on predefined client criteria. And some recruiters get close to their candidates and meet them all in person; others do not.

Recruiters and sometimes even hedge funds post opportunities on job listing sites, including monster.com, hotjobs.com, and careerbuilder.com. The Association for Investment Management and Research also maintains an active job posting section on its Web site (www.cfainstitute.org) for its members. An additional resource is Bloomberg's job site, where recruiters and hedge funds also post opportunities. However, a Bloomberg terminal is need-

D Recruiters

ed to access these job postings.

Finally, there are numerous hedge fund industry conferences that hedge fund personnel and recruiters attend, but it would be wise to conduct due diligence on the conferences before attending. Many are attended primarily by third-party suppliers and vendors to hedge funds, such as law firms, software providers, and accounting firms. Hedge fund investment professionals do attend investment banking/prime brokerage conferences on a regular basis.

D | Recruiters

E

RESUMES

Crafting a Resume

Crafting a solid resume is an important step in attracting the attention of a hedge fund manager or trader. The resumes in this section provide examples of what PMs and traders will respond to positively. The resumes are organized according to particular job opportunities, but they all exhibit many of the following characteristics.

Postitive Resume Characteristics

EXPERIENCE:

☐ Hedge fund or asset management experience (internships)

☐ The CFA designation, provided by the Association for Investment Management and Research (AIMR). CFA is a good indicator of interest in investing

☐ Recognized excellence in some area of academics, leadership, professional career

FOCUS:

☐ Emphasis on valuation work and modeling skills (for Analysts)

☐ De-emphasis on transactions volume and/or number of deals closed (especially pertinent for investment bankers)

SIMPLICITY:

☐ No job experience should contain more than five main points (bullet points) except when listing representative deal experience

☐ Font, format, punctuation must be simple, clean and consistent. No need to highlight words/phrases in italics, bold, etc.

CHARACTER:

☐ Integrity is critical. Do not exaggerate achievements, personal or professional or relating to personal investing

☐ Account for all time since graduation from college, there should be no missing gaps of more than three months

☐ Make use of Personal section at bottom of resume to note interests and hobbies. Personality should come through in this section

The following resumes are organized into six categories based on six sample job opportunities:

1) **JOB 1:** ANALYST: Value Long/Short Fund

2) **JOB 2:** ANALYST: Long/Short Market Neutral Fund

3) **JOB 3:** ANALYST: Multistrategy Fund

4) **JOB 4:** ANALYST: Event-Driven/Special Situations Fund

5) **JOB 5:** JUNIOR TRADER: Global Macro Fund

6) **JOB 6:** TRADER: Event-Driven Fund

Note: Names of candidates, universities, and employment firms have been given three-letter acronyms (i.e., ABC University) or have been given generic names (i.e., Large Investment Bank).

ANALYST: Value Long/Short Fund

CANDIDATE CRITERIA	• Passion for public markets, value investor • 2+ years experience

Sample Job

COMPANY PROFILE	Several hundred million dollar hedge fund employs a fundamental bottoms-up value approach to investing in U.S. equities.
JOB DESCRIPTION	The firm seeks a highly motivated Analyst to support PMs.
JOB REQUIREMENTS	• MUST BE passionate about the public markets and MUST BE a value investor • MUST BE from a top undergraduate program • MUST HAVE excellent Excel skills, including strong knowledge of macros. • MUST HAVE at least 2 years of investment banking or research analyst experience in basic industries; also 1+ years of PUBLIC SECTOR BUY SIDE EXPERIENCE A PLUS. Would also consider consultants who have a keen interest in the public markets • Start date will be September/October 2006 • MUST HAVE top valuation and Excel skills
COMPENSATION	Competitive base plus bonus

E | Resumes

STRONG POINTS	● **Representative versus full list of transactions categorized by deal type** ● **Academic achievement** ● **CFA designation**

William Taft
Address
Phone numbers (home/cell), (work)
email

Experience
LARGE LBO FIRM
Associate, *Restructuring and Reorganization Group, July 2004 – Present*
Analyst, *Restructuring and Reorganization Group, July 2001 – July 2004*
Advise distressed companies, creditors and institutions in special situations. Negotiate and create restructuring proposals including the structuring of bank debt, high-yield bonds, preferred equity, common equity, warrants and options. Advise clients on capital and performance budgeting, Chapter 11 alternatives, employee compensation programs and divestiture options. Develop business plans and in-depth integrated operating models to evaluate restructuring and operational scenarios. Perform valuations using discounted cash flow, comparable company and comparable transaction analyses. Involved in merger and acquisition advisory activity. Draft confidential offering memoranda and solicit capital for exit and project financings.

Representative Transactions

- *Company restructuring advisory*. Current and completed company restructuring advisory assignments include: ABC, DEF, GHI, JKL, MNO, PQR and STU.
- *Creditor restructuring advisory*. Current and completed creditor restructuring advisory assignments include: the secured creditors of VWX and the unsecured creditors of YZA.
- *M&A advisory*. Sale of BCD to the EFG and sale of certain non-core assets including HIJ. Sale of various BCD assets including power plants, an oil and gas exploration and production company and an international paper manufacturer.
- *General corporate finance advisory*. Advised the Board of Directors of HIJ on strategic alternatives relating to potential shareholder litigation from largest shareholder.

BOUTIQUE INVESTMENT BANK
Summer Intern, *Leveraged Finance Group, May 2000 - August 2000*
Worked as a summer generalist in the leveraged finance group that included bank debt origination, high yield bond origination and financial sponsor coverage. Kept group abreast of activity and pricing in the leveraged loan market. Solicited new business, researched potential LBO targets, performed various valuation exercises and prepared deal memoranda.

Representative transactions include:

- *Leveraged buyout:* KLM on the acquisition of NOP, Inc., a maker of telecommunication towers.
- *Loan origination and syndication:* Structured a $250 million leveraged loan for QRS.
- *Secondary loan trading:* Sold $50 million participation in loan backing TUV's leveraged buyout of WXY.

Education
ZAB University, May 2001
Bachelor of Science in Finance and Accounting with Minor in History, *magna cum laude*. GPA – 3.8. Elected Vice-Chairperson of the Student Activities Board; responsible for all university club life and club budget allocation. First baseman on the Baseball Team. Founder and President of large club; awarded club of the year in 1996 and 1997. Member of the President's Community Service Team. Vice President of Investment Society. Vice President of Finance Society.

Honors: Named University Scholar and awarded trips to the Netherlands, Belgium, England, Italy and Spain. Elected Beta Gamma Sigma (undergraduate business equivalent of Phi Beta Kappa), President's Service Award for Leadership, Founder's Day Scholar, Golden Torch Award for Leadership, President's Award for Volunteer Service, Dean's Honor Key and Dean's Honor Roll (every semester).

Professional Certifications
CFA Level III Candidate, Series 7, Series 63

Community Involvement
Boys and Girls Republic tutoring program for professionals; Founder and Tutor.

Personal
Black Belt in Judo. Lifeguard and Water Safety Instructor. PADI certified scuba diver. Enjoy team sports, traveling and food.

STRONG POINTS	• **Hedge fund experience/internship**
	• **Emphasis on valuation, de-emphasis on transactions volume**
	• **Simple, clean format with no more than five bullet points per job**

Benjamin Harrison
Address
Phone numbers (home/cell), (work)
email

EDUCATION

2004 – 2006
ABC UNIVERSITY
Candidate for Master in Business Administration degree, June 2005. President of the Investment Club.

1994 – 1998
DEF COLLEGE
Bachelor of Science in Business, Finance Concentration.

EXPERIENCE

Summer 2004
LARGE HEDGE FUND
Summer Analyst
Evaluated investments for $400 million value-oriented hedge fund. Analyzed special situations including spin-offs and equity stubs, and value and equity/debt investments in stressed and distressed companies in a variety of industries in the U.S. and U.K.

2000 - 2003
PRIVATE EQUITY FIRM, NEW YORK, NY
Associate
- Analyze investment opportunities and monitor investments for $1.0+ billion private equity fund.
- Evaluate potential investments in business outsourcing, insurance, food and beverage, and healthcare industries.
- Championed, conducted due diligence on, and supported $75 million investment in insurance firm and $150 million investment in pub operating company.
- Monitor control position in European food and beverage company and sold business to management team.

1999 – 2000 **BOUTIQUE INVESTMENT BANK, NEW YORK, NY**
Media & Telecommunications Group, Financial Analyst
- Responsibilities included a variety of financial and valuation analyses for companies in the media and telecommunications industries.
- Experience included valuation analyses, extensive modeling, evaluation of strategic and financing structures, drafting of private placement memoranda and SEC documents and participation in due diligence activities in connection with the execution of equity, high yield and merger and acquisition transactions.
- Selected Deal Experience: Concurrent $450MM High Yield/ $130MM Convertible Preferred Offerings; $160MM IPO and Strategic Advisory.

1998 – 1999 **SMALL FINANCIAL SERVICES FIRM, NEW YORK, NY**
Analyst, Investment Consulting Group
- Performed range of financial analyses for anticipated transactions in chemical, machinery, and semiconductor industries; valuation analysis included discounted cash flow and trading multiples, and acquisition multiples.
- Marketed firm's risk-management capabilities to various top-tier financial services firms.

Personal: Fluent in Japanese. Enjoy playing the piano, reading, snowboarding, camping and basketball.

Resumes

E

STRONG POINTS	• Focus on valuation work
	• Alignment of personal interests, extracurriculars, and professional experience
	• Academic and professional achievement

John Adams
Address
Phone numbers (home/cell), (work)
email

Experience
LARGE INVESTMENT BANK, New York, NY, 6/04-Present
Associate
Promoted to Associate in June of 2003 after working as an Analyst in the group for two years (the first second year Analyst promotion in Investment Banking Department since 1999).

Financial Analyst, 7/02-6/04
One of two first-year Analysts selected by firm's private equity fund. Worked closely with fund partners, co-investors and other firm professionals in evaluating and executing investments. Extensive interaction with company management teams.
Participate in all aspects of private equity transactions, including:
- Screening and evaluating potential investment opportunities
- Performing relevant financial analysis and valuation using a range of methodologies including LBO, DCF, sum-of-the-parts, comparable public company and precedent transaction analsyses.
- Drafting and negotiating of term sheets
- Structuring investments throughout the capital structure, primarily convertible and equivalent securities · Coordinating with legal counsel and outside accountants
- Working with management of companies to prepare budgets and financial analyses

Representative assignments:
- Worked on various transaction types including growth situations, leveraged buyouts, recapitalizations and corporate orphans
- Evaluated investments in several industries including: automotive parts, consumer credit, specialty retail, value-added resellers (VARS), embedded computers, RF engineering service providers
- Appointed as an observer to the Board of Directors of DEF

Deals include the following:
- GHI: lead investor in first and second round financing of RF engineering services firm. Acquired by JKL in August of 2003
- MNO: co-investor in first round financing of Austrian facilities-based application service provider founded by a highly successful telecommunications entrepreneur
- PQR: co-investor in second round financing of European Internet incubator

Education
ABC UNIVERSITY
Bachelor of Science in Economics, May 2002
- Cum Laude graduate with a concentration in Finance
- Cumulative GPA: 3.63/4.00
- Elected member of University's student governing body
- Teaching Assistant, Finance Department
- Other: DEF Rush Chair 2001-2002

Personal
1999-Present
- Interests: investing (value-oriented strategy), guitar, swimming, basketball
- Active, contributing member of online investors club
  - ➢ In 2004 won $2,500 prize for investment idea of the week
- Weekly mentor and SAT tutor to a Brooklyn high school student

CANDIDATE CRITERIA	●Industry generalist, value investing philosophy ●3+ years experience

Sample Job

COMPANY PROFILE	$1+ Billion hedge fund with strong track record and hard-core fundamental value investment style and market neutral orientation. Firm focuses on small and mid-cap investments.
JOB DESCRIPTION	Firm seeks an Analyst to join its Investment Team. The Analyst will be working under the Portfolio Manager, helping to maintain current positions as well as research new investment ideas for the Portfolio.
JOB REQUIREMENTS	●MUST HAVE a MINIMUM of 3 years experience in investment banking or equity research with superior valuation skills. Private Equity experience that includes solid deal exposure to the public markets is also applicable. ●MUST HAVE a value investing philosophy and an intense due diligence oriented, bottoms-up approach to investing. ●MUST HAVE experience in more than one industry. Firm seeks generalists. ●MUST HAVE top academic background.
COMPENSATION	Competitive base plus bonus

Resumes

E

STRONG POINTS	• **Asset management experience/internship** • **Focus on valuation and modeling skills** • **Professional achievement**

James Monroe
Address
Phone numbers (home/cell), (work)
email

Work Experience

Leading Investment Bank, New York, NY
Mergers and Acquisitions Group – Analyst
July 2003 to Present

- Offered a 3rd year in the M&A group (top 10% of class)
- Named to the Analytics and Modeling Committee responsible for group-wide templates
- Active member of University ABC recruiting team
- Proficient in valuation and merger analyses including: comparable company and transaction analysis, accretion / dilution, joint venture, discounted cash flow and leveraged buy-out
- Advised on the following announced transactions:
  - ➢ DEF on its merger with GHI Foods
  - ➢ JKL on its purchase of MNO
  - ➢ PQR on its strategic investment with STU
  - ➢ VWX on the renewal of its shareholders rights plan
  - ➢ YZA on the placement of private equity

Large Asset Management Firm, New York, NY
Prime Funds Portfolio Group - Intern
May 2002 to Aug. 2002

- Performed credit analysis and made investment recommendations for an $10 billion High Yield Bond and Bank Debt fund
- Chairman of the Interns' Committee, Valedictory Speaker at the end of summer ceremonies
- Completed training courses in Option Theory, Futures, Portfolio Investing and Advanced Excel

Investment Bank Private Client, Winston-Salem, NC
High Net Worth Consulting Group - Intern
May 2001 to Aug. 2001

- Worked on a consulting team to devise investment strategies for high net worth individuals

Education

ABC University
Bachelor of Arts – Major GPA: 3.4
Sept. 1999 to May 2003

- Major in International Relations, concentrating in International Finance
- DEF History honors society

The GHI School
Summa Cum Laude – SAT: Verbal 780, Math 700
Aug. 1995 to June 1999

Personal

The JKL Foundation for Education, **New York, NY**
Chairman and Founder

- Raising capital to aid the un-funded pre-K programs in regional Charter Schools
  Helping Tomorrow, **New York, NY**
  Volunteer and Big Brother in the HelpUSA charity program
- Actively coordinate fund raising events and participate in service programs to benefit underprivileged families
  Junior Achievements Program, **New York, NY**
  Volunteer Teacher to second grade students at The MNO School

STRONG POINTS	• Hedge fund experience/internship
	• Academic achievement
	• Alignment of academic coursework, extracurriculars, and professional experience

James Madison
Address
Phone numbers (home/cell), (work)
email

Experience

LEADING LBO FUND, NEW YORK, NY, 2004-present
Vice President

- Identify, evaluate, and execute principal investment opportunities for a $1 billion buyout fund. Advise senior management of portfolio companies on potential acquisitions, financings, and corporate strategy.
- Closed a $52 million follow-on convertible preferred investment into a communications semiconductor company. Helped negotiate two credit agreement amendments, take-or-pay manufacturing agreement, and foundry transition agreement.
- Closed a $120 million convertible preferred investment into a food processing firm. Integrally involved in every phase of transaction from preliminary evaluation through wind down.
- Evaluated LBO/corporate carve-out of alarm company ABC from DEF and subsequent sale six months later to GHI.
- Led industry due diligence that resulted in growth financing of biosolids manager JKL. Participated on team that reviewed and executed $200 million buyout and integration of largest competitor from MNO.
- Individually evaluated and made investment recommendations on dozens of potential transactions.

LARGE HEDGE FUND. NEW YORK, NY, Summer 2003
Associate

- Long/Short, special situations value-oriented fund with $1B in assets.
- Focus on variety of special situations in both equity and distressed debt as well as traditional long/short value strategies across several industries. Very research intensive approach with the primary goal of capital preservation.

LEADING LBO FIRM, NEW YORK, NY, 2000-2002
Analyst

- Analyzed and executed principal investment opportunities. Actively involved in monitoring operational and financial performance, providing strategic advice, devising financial targets linked to management compensation and evaluating exit strategies.
- Closed a $450 million leveraged buyout of an operator of cardiac hospitals. Helped negotiate merger, stock option, employment, and credit agreements. Authored bank marketing documents.
- Analyzed and executed principal investment transactions. Advised corporate clients on merger, acquisition, and restructuring opportunities.
- Closed a $200 million joint venture leveraged buyout of a pub operator.
- Closed a $220 million joint venture leveraged buyout of a leasing company operator.
- Closed a $180 million leveraged recapitalization of a manufacturer of mobile homes.

Education

ABC University, MBA, 2002 -2004
Member of Investment Club, Member of Comedy Club, staff writer for Business School newspaper

DEF University, 1995-1999
The Business Honors Program
Bachelor of Business Administration
Majors: Business Honors & Finance
Major GPA: 4.0/4.0; Overall GPA: 3.8/4.0

Personal:

Competitive runner, avid Asian art collector, enjoy Kung-fu movies

E | Resumes

STRONG POINTS	• **Asset management experience/internship**
	• **Academic achievement**
	• **Focus on valuation skills and selected versus full transaction experience**

Stacey Lincoln
Address
Phone numbers (home/cell), (university)
email

Education
ABC UNIVERSITY, September 2005 – Present
MBA Candidate, June 2006
Activities: Finance & Investments Club
                        Student Association Development Committee

DEF UNIVERSITY
Bachelor of Science in Economics, May 2001
Dual Majors in Finance and Strategic Management, Minor in English.
GPA: 3.9/4.0. GMAT: 760/800

Activities: *President & Founder*, GHI Club. *Alumnae Chairperson*, JKL Honor Society.

                        Social Events / Formals Chairperson, University Sorority

Experience
LARGE ASSET MANAGEMENT FIRM, NY

Summer Associate, Investment Group, *Summer 2005*

- Analyzed public equities in the consumer appliances industry, culminating in a comprehensive industry review detailing investment recommendations.
- Conducted investment diligence including detailed industry research, valuation analysis and management interviews. Assessed industry outlook including fundamental changes, channel and customer checks, macroeconomic drivers, valuation metrics and corporate strategies.

LARGE PRIVATE EQUITY FIRM, CA, 2002 – 2005
Private Equity Associate
- Review potential investments: conduct extensive financial, business, accounting, legal, environmental and industry due diligence on potential transactions. Evaluate the quality of business models and management teams, develop a thorough understanding of a particular industry and develop projections upon which to evaluate the returns of the investment.

Selected Transaction Experience:
- $400 million leveraged recapitalization of MNO, a communications semiconductor company.
- $50 million platform build-up of PQR, a digital media firm created in partnership with STU.

TOP TIER INVESTMENT BANK, INVESTMENT BANKING DIVISION**,** NY

Financial Analyst, Mergers & Acquisitions Department, *2001 – 2002*
Summer Financial Analyst, *Summer 2000*

- Built comprehensive financial models including merger plans, leveraged buyout, leveraged recapitalization, discounted cash flow, spin-off, and comparable company and transactions analyses
- Performed and coordinated comprehensive diligence on a variety of transactions
- Prepared client and board presentation materials, confidential selling memoranda, roadshow and management presentations, internal committee memoranda and sales force marketing materials
- Analyst captain for summer intern training – responsible for leading technical training of summer analyst class

Selected Transaction Experience:
- Advisory for VWX in the acquisition of YZA ($2.7Bn), which created the second largest copper company in the world; performed valuation and pro forma analyses for simultaneous hostile bids for BCD and VWX.
- Advisory for EFG in the acquisition of HIJ ($1.2Bn), which created the largest title insurance company in the United States; created pro forma models, structured transaction to satisfy insurance regulators and credit agencies.
- $200 million follow-on equity offering for KLM Corporation.
- $250 million senior debt facility for NOP Properties.

Resumes
E

CANDIDATE CRITERIA	• Top academic (college) credentials, strong interest in public markets • 0-2 years experience

Sample Job

COMPANY PROFILE	Top-tier and top performing multibillion dollar multistrategy hedge fund. Staff of approximately 75 globally.
JOB DESCRIPTION	Firm's SF office seeks highly motivated Analyst.
JOB REQUIREMENTS	• MUST HAVE NO MORE THAN 2 YEARS from Investment Bank, or from buy-side firm • MUST have graduated from College/University with TOP GPA (>3.7), and top SAT scores • MUST DEMONSTRATE strong interest in public sector investing • MUST HAVE very strong work ethic and strong desire to learn.
COMPENSATION	Competitive base plus bonus

Resumes

E

STRONG POINTS	• **Hedge fund experience/internship** • **Academic achievement** • **CFA candidate** • **Simple, clean format**

Warren Harding
Address
Phone numbers (home/cell), (work)
email

EDUCATION

ABC University, May 2005
Magna cum Laude *(GPA 3.65/4.00)*
Concentrations in Operations Research, Statistics, Management, and Systems Engineering
- *Honors*: Beta Gamma Sigma, Golden Key International Honor Society, Dean's List
- *Primary Activities*: Vice-President, DEF Fraternity; Member, Varsity Sprint Football Team

EXPERIENCE

DEF Associates, New York, NY
Equity Analyst, Summer 2004
- Identified event-driven opportunities within the large-cap value universe for a $250 million+ market-neutral hedge fund
- Evaluated perceived equity mispricings in a combined statistical/fundamental framework and through extensive interviews with company management, sell-side equity analysts, and industry experts
- Prepared and presented investment theses in food & beverages, retail, banking, and defense sectors
- Created an accounting model to monitor pair wise fundamental relationships on a historical basis, and several smaller, supplemental models for off-balance sheet liabilities such as defined-benefit pension plans and dilutive securities
- Devised a set of potential flags for companies with suspicious or aggressive accounting practices such as reductions in receivables allowances, capitalizations of operating expenses, income from non-recurring sources, and other forms of earnings manipulation

Analyst, Quantitative Strategies, Summer 2003
- Developed proprietary, computer-based trading models for various domestic equity strategies
- Performed quantitative market research to ascertain equity return patterns and evaluate historical risk
- Worked on multi-disciplinary team towards the creation of cross-sectional model covering the energy sector

New York Giants, New York, NY
Analyst, Special Projects, May 2002–May 2003
- Participated in the construction of a computational model to analyze League fourth-down decision-making
- Designed an Excel-based statistical prototype which constituted the architecture of the final product
- Built an exhaustive database and a series of payoff functions to determine League performance measures

ADDITIONAL INFORMATION
- CFA Level II Candidate
- Extensive programming experience in Visual Basic, Matlab, and QA
- Interests include literature, squash, basketball, and tennis
- Proficient in Spanish

E

Resumes

STRONG POINTS	• **Focus on valuation skills and deal structure exposure** • **Alignment of personal interests, coursework, & professional experience** • **Personable characteristics**

Zachary Taylor
Address
Phone numbers (home/cell), (work)
email

WORK EXPERIENCE

Large Investment Bank, New York, NY   *July 2004 – Present*
Associate, Mergers & Acquisitions
- Supervised and participated in the valuation analysis, strategic review and modeling exercises for various transactions in the consumer products, food and beverage, aerospace and defense, forest products and chemicals industries.
- Proficient in a variety of deal structures including LBOs, asset sales/swaps, stock and cash deals and experienced in valuation methodologies such as comparable company and precedent transaction analysis, DCF and sum of parts analysis.
- Prepared information memorandums, board presentations and fairness opinions. Participated in the drafting of merger proxies, engagement letters and other legal documents related to the M&A process.

Selected Deal Experience:
- *Advised ABC on its sale to DEF for $20 billion:* Following a rapid decline in ABC's stock price, the company viewed the transaction as a way to preserve remaining shareholder value. Weeks after announcement, DEF opted not to pursue the deal because of information uncovered in their diligence process.
- *Advised GHI on the divestiture of approximately $7.0 billion of assets:* As part of the JKL/GHI merger, the DOJ required cellular properties with overlapping licenses to be divested to satisfy FCC requirements. The three part transaction consisted of a $4.6 billion asset swap with MNO and the sale of $2.4 billion in cellular assets to PQR and STU Communications.
- *Advised VWX on the $685 million purchase of MNO business:* In VWX's first significant acquisition, it became the world's leading supplier of solid propulsion systems.
- *Advised YZA on the purchase of $1.7 billion in assets from BCD:* YZA sought high quality paper mills to increase its U.S. presence and overall size.
- *Sold assets of EFG to HIJ as part of a $4.0 billion, 5 year manufacturing supply agreement:* EFG sold these assets as part of its strategy shift towards a virtual manufacturing/outsourcing model.
- *Defense advisor for HIJ following KLM $1.5 billion hostile takeover offer:* KLM sought to increase its Latin American presence through an acquisition of HIJ which was trading at significantly depressed levels prior to the offer. As defense advisor, an additional $640 million in value was extracted from KLM and the offer transformed into a friendly transaction.
- *Advised NOP on the purchase of $390 million in assets from QRS:* To complete the company's planned national footprint of 39 GHz spectrum and fixed broadband wireless platform, NOP acquired the license portfolio of QRS.
- *Advised TUV on its $960 million attempted hostile takeover of WXY:* TUV sought to acquire WXY as well as ZAB, which was 71% owned by WXY at the time. TUV was a shareholder in both companies prior to the takeover offer and sought to breakup the two firms believing there was no strategic fit between them.

Boutique Investment Bank, New York, NY   *May 2003 – August 2003*
Analyst
- Worked on sell-side transactions representing companies in deals with financial sponsors and strategic acquirers.
- Performed company valuations, market research for idea generation and had interaction with private equity investors.

Large Investment Bank New York, NY   *November 2002 – May 2003*
Investment Banking Analyst
- Helped develop and maintain financial models in the investment banking group for LBO analysis, M&A transactions and debt and equity financing.
- Provided support for the investment banking team and assisted the Global Technologies Group in developing and testing new models based on in-house developed applications.

EDUCATION
ABC University, B.S. in Finance and International Business.
Class of May 2003 GPA 3.5/4.0, Member of Dean's List, Graduated Cum Laude.

PERSONAL
Active investor since 1999. Interests include mountain biking, art and currently training in classical piano.

Resumes

E

CANDIDATE CRITERIA	● M & A valuation skills, strong interest in public markets ● 2+ years experience

Sample Job

COMPANY PROFILE	Event-driven hedge fund was founded in 1991 and focuses on merger arbitrage, restructurings, spin-offs and bankruptcies. The firm currently employs a staff of 13.
JOB DESCRIPTION	Firm seeks Hedge Fund Research Analyst.
JOB REQUIREMENTS	● AT LEAST 2 years relevant experience in M&A, merger arbitrage, restructurings, spin-offs and/or bankruptcies. ● MUST HAVE strong valuation and communication skills and the ability to analyze a security and reach a conclusion in a quick time frame. ● MUST HAVE a strong interest in the markets and the desire to work in an environment that emphasizes teamwork.
COMPENSATION	Competitive base plus bonus

E

Resumes

STRONG POINTS	• **Academic achievement** • **Focus on valuation skills** • **Personable characteristics**

John Tyler
Address
Phone numbers (home/cell), (work)
email

EXPERIENCE

LARGE INVESTMENT BANK, New York, NY, 7/04-Present
Investment Banking Analyst – Technology Mergers and Acquisitions Group
- Performed and drafted valuation, due diligence and marketing materials for buy/sell-side situations within the technology universe
- Performed due diligence and extensive financial analysis for structuring M&A deals, including accretion/dilution, contribution analysis, exchange ratio/ownership analysis, and interlopers' ability to pay. Applied various valuation methods based on comparable company analysis, precedent transaction analysis, sum of the parts valuation, and DCF
- Built three statement merger consequence models. Assisted clients in building their operating models
- Prepared board presentations, defense profiles, fairness opinion materials, engagement letters, CIMs, and data room
- Selected transactions include:
  - ABC's acquisition of DEF *(closed)*
  - $300 million sale of an electronic money transfer provider *(closed)*
  - Raised $25 million of second round private investment for a CRM software company
  - $1 billion merger between semiconductor chip packaging companies in Southeast Asia and the United States
  - Worked on multiple leveraged buyout transactions including a $3 billion buyout of an electronics manufacturer, plus other LBOs in the communications equipment and business services industries
  - $350 million sale of an IT consulting company
  - Restructuring of distressed telecommunications company

LARGE INVESTMENT BANK, San Francisco, CA, 6/03-8/03
Investment Banking Summer Analyst - Technology Group
- Served as lead analyst for the follow-on offering of *GHI* compared the pro forma earnings impact and credit statistics between equity and straight debt/convertible debt issuance
- Assisted in the roadshow and the creation of sales memo of *JKL*

LARGE ASSET MANAGEMENT FIRM, New York, NY, 5/02-8/02
International Accounting Summer Analyst
- Analyzed balance sheet to determine the effects of translation, asset reclasses, depreciation, and tax vs. book differences
- Introduced an automated quarterly financial reporting package by integrating Excel & Access through complex queries
- Created journal entries for inter-company annual P&L closeout of foreign subsidiaries to conform to US GAAP
- Used job costing to allocate monthly revenues and expenses from revenue generating departments to support divisions

EDUCATION

MNO University, 9/00-6/04
College of Arts and Sciences: **Bachelor of Arts – Double major in International Studies and Asian and Middle Eastern Studies**
  - GPA in School of Business Administration: 3.8/4.0
  - Graduation with High Distinction
  - Emphases in Finance and Accounting
  - BBA Membership and Relations, Asian Business Association

Related Experience and Activities included:
MNO University, 9/00-6/04
Organizer of PQR Tour of Japan/Vice President/1st violinist
- Assisted MNO in strengthening its presence in Japan and its cooperation with the leading Japanese University
- Liaison for the Japanese Ministry of Culture and Media; organized three concerts in Tokyo
- Served as MC in both Japanese and English at major concert with an attendance of 500 people
- Arranged all logistics, including marketing, travel itinerary, insurance, and accommodations for 90 participants

MNO University
9/99-6/03
Columnist: Wrote "Letters from Japan" about study abroad; writer for the Opinion section

PERSONAL

Languages/Interests: Fluently read, write, and speak Japanese; competitive tennis player for 12 years, enjoy golf, basketball, rollerblading, karaoke, and travel

Resumes

E

STRONG POINTS	• **Academic excellence** • **Leadership experience** • **Simple, clean format**

Franklin Pierce
Address
Phone numbers (home/cell), (work)
email

EXPERIENCE
Top-tier Investment Bank, New York, NY
Associate, **Merger and Strategic Advisory Group, Investment Banking Division 2004 – 2005**
- o Advised ABC Holdings on the sale of DEF Company GHI. Performed valuation analysis, assisted in preparing the offering memorandum and managed prospective buyers through various stages of the process.
- o Advised JKL on a public equity offering. Performed valuation analysis, participated in drafting the prospectus and prepared materials for the internal approval process. Worked closely with legal counsel and JKL management.
- o Advised MNO on a high yield bond offering. Participated in drafting the offering memorandum, prepared materials for presentation to investors and worked with internal high yield capital markets during the transaction.
- o Advised PQR on its unsolicited bid to acquire STU. Analyzed target and acquirer shareholder bases, performed due diligence at a client site and performed market research.
- o Prepared materials in client service of a retail company with approximately $9 billion in annual revenue. Performed valuation analysis, researched the retail sector and prepared various presentations.
- o Participated actively in analyst recruiting at VWX University.

Large Investment Bank. New York, NY
Summer Associate, **Consumer / Retail Investment Banking Group (Summer 2003)**
- o Prepared materials for presentation to senior level management, assisted in performing valuation analysis and performed market research to develop strategic alternatives for consumer products companies.

U.S. Navy, Charleston, SC
Lieutenant, USS Klakring, 1999 - 2003
Managed divisions of up to 50 personnel onboard a forward-deployed guided-missile frigate. Duties included Combat Information Center Officer, Navigation Officer, and Auxiliaries Engineering Officer.

Instructor - **Physics Division, Enlisted Department** (1999)
- o Taught physics to enlisted personnel. Subject matter taught includes basic nuclear physics.

EDUCATION
YZA, **Graduate School of Business**
Master of Business Administration, June 2004
Graduated with Honors
Writing published in several publications
Investment banking career advisor
Dean's Student Admission Committee

VWX University
Bachelor of Science in Engineering, Civil and Environmental Engineering, May 1998
GPA: 3.8 / 4.0; Phi Beta Kappa; Tau Beta Pi; Magna cum Laude
Intramural basketball; Washington, D.C. community service trip; physics tutor

STRONG POINTS	• Hedge fund experience/internship • Academic excellence • Focus on valuation skills and deal structure exposure

Jennifer McKinley
Address
Phone numbers (home/cell), (work)
email

Education
ABC University, 2004 - 2006
Candidate for Master in Business Administration degree, June 2006.
Member of Investment, Healthcare and Golf Clubs.

DEF University, May 1999
Bachelor of Science degree in Finance, with Honors.

Experience
HEDGE FUND, New York, NY, Summer 2005
Research Analyst
- Market neutral fund focused mainly on long/short value stocks, event-driven, and special situations, in a number of different sectors including healthcare, medical devices, retail and pharmaceuticals.
- Conducted extensive research in retail materializing into thirty-five self-generated investments on both the long and the short side that contributed to achieving a 10% overall fund return in the first quarter of 2003.

LEADING PRIVATE EQUITY FIRM, New York, NY, 2001 – 2004
Associate
- One of 15 professionals investing $2+ billion of private capital at a leading private equity firm; firm manages over 50 portfolio companies. Responsibilities included sourcing, analyzing, recommending and executing new investments. Evaluated industries and businesses using fundamental bottoms-up research, leading to development of investment theses. Proactively contacted, recruited and evaluated potential partner CEOs and senior executives. Executed leveraged transactions with primary responsibility for all business due diligence, financial modeling and valuation work, deal structuring and transaction negotiation. Assisted with portfolio company monitoring; advised management teams on strategic and financial issues.
- GHI - closed $100 million commitment to provider of specialty pharmacy services. Researched industry, developed investment thesis and identified/recruited management team. Executed $42 million MBO of JKL Services; closed an $18 million acquisition of an oncology pharmacy. Raised senior bank debt.
- MNO - completed $180 million corporate carve-out of a third-party provider of electronic funds transfer services and subsequent $25 million tuck-in acquisition. Structured and negotiated firm investments.
- Portfolio company management responsibilities for PQR; STU (restructuring); and WXY (incremental equity investment, management changes).
- Strategic Development Work - Hedge Funds. With 2 senior partners, led efforts to develop the strategy and business plan for a liquid alternative asset management business at firm. Recruited asset management executives and portfolio managers. Cultivated relationships with prime brokers. Analyzed several potential business structures.

LARGE INVESTMENT BANK, NEW YORK, NY, 1999 – 2001
Financial Analyst, Mergers & Acquisitions Group
- Analyzed and executed an array of strategic transactions and investments, including, mergers, acquisitions, leveraged buyouts, joint ventures, divestitures and restructurings on behalf of U.S. and international clients. Responsibilities included developing and building financial models and valuation analyses, authoring client presentations and internal committee memoranda, managing due diligence processes and overseeing the work of Analysts and Associates.
- Advised ZAB on its white knight acquisition of CDE Corporation ($13.6 billion).
- Advised FGH on its acquisition of IJK and LMN ($425 million).
- Advised OPQ on its acquisition of RST ($75 million).
- Advised UVW on its acquisition of XYZ ($330 million).
- Advised ABC on its merger with DEF, Ltd. ($615 million).

Personal
Interests include reading, travel, investing.

E | Resumes

CANDIDATE CRITERIA	• Strong work ethic, extreme attention to detail • Series 7, 63 when hired

Sample Job

COMPANY PROFILE	Privately held alternative asset management firm based in Manhattan. Founded over 15 years ago, the Firm has had outstanding risk-adjusted performance and has among the longest track records in the alternative investment industry. The firm manages combined assets of several billion dollars in an internal hedge fund and through its multi-manager business.
JOB DESCRIPTION	Firm seeks an entry-level trader to work with $60M Macro fund that trades currencies and commodities. The Junior Trader will be responsible for running commands using established programs.
JOB REQUIREMENTS	• MUST HAVE a very strong work ethic, extreme attention to detail, and be willing to do what it takes to make the group successful. • MUST HAVE a solid academic background. College degree should have some emphasis on statistics/mathematics. • MUST HAVE excellent Excel skills, including strong knowledge of macros. • Hours are approximately 7:30am to 5:30pm, but the Jr. Trader will be on call 24/7 for work emergencies and business needs. • Candidate will be required to pass the Series 7, 63 when hired.
COMPENSATION	Competitive base plus bonus

E Resumes

STRONG POINTS	● **Trading experience** ● **Trading system skills** ● **Academic achievement**

James Carter
Address
Phone numbers (home/ cell), (work)
email

Education:
ABC University
2001-2005. B.Sc. in Mathematics with Computer Science. Overall GPA: 3.80.
SAT Math: 800; SAT Verbal: 770.
Relevant Coursework: Finance Theory; Stochastic Processes; Discrete Mathematics for Computer Science; Probability Theory; Algorithms; Microeconomics; Game Theory; Laboratory in Software Engineering (conducted in Java); Object Oriented Programming; Differential Equations; Linear Algebra; Multivariable Calculus.
Activities: Candidate for CFA Level I Program, May 2004 (still awaiting results).
College: Member of the Division I Varsity Heavyweight Rowing Team, ABC Model
United Nations Team, and President of 2002 Community Service Committee.
Distinctions: Member of the DEF Program, Class of 2001. Finished 1st out of 195 students in Finance Theory in December 2001. Graduated 1st in class of 300 from GHI Secondary School.

Experience:
JKL Investment Managers   *New York, NY*
Trader Assistant, 2005 - Present
· Assist in risk management of a diversified treasury options position
· Manage daily account balancing and reconciliation activities
· Study options pricing theory and application in depth
· Execute trades on multiple platforms (Eurex, Globex, Simex)

MNO   *New York, NY*
Summer 2004. Worked in Strategic Development division in the Private Client department. Analyzed figures for transactional revenues, seasoned attrition, bad debt expense, and various other categories for trends and correlations. Wrote reports to explain findings, and made presentations to senior level management to describe how these trends and correlations can be used to explain past performance. Identified troubling trends that may be a forecast for low future earnings, and presented this to MNO's management.

PQR   *New York, NY*
Summer 2003. Created an online Change Request Application using ASP, VBScript, and some JavaScript. Allowed PQR employees to update, add, delete and view their own records in a database from anywhere in the world through the Web. Allowed managers to access their employees' records through the Web, and allowed employees to view other employees' records through the Web.

STU   *Cambridge, MA*
Summer 2002. Created Microsoft Access database from Internet files and Excel spreadsheets. Wrote simple SQL queries to analyze and sort the database, and automated the database using Visual Basic modules.

Skills:
Computer skills: Proficient with Excel VBA, Java, SQL, HTML, Unix, ASP, VBScript, Microsoft Access, Microsoft Excel.
Language skills: French and Hindi adequately.

Awards:
January 2001
1 of 12 selected to sit on the National Editorial Advisory Committee country's largest youth magazine.

Resumes

E

STRONG POINTS	• **Trading-related experience**
	• **Academic achievement**
	• **Alignment of course-work and professional experience**

Millard Fillmore
Address
Phone numbers (home/ cell), (work)
email

EDUCATION

ABC University   May 2005
Bachelor of Business Administration – Graduate with High Honors
Major: Finance
Overall GPA: 3.91   Major GPA: 3.88
Financed 100% of education through summer savings and scholarships
o   Completed two graduate courses in Fixed Income & Financial Derivatives
  o   Modeled after all 3 levels of CFA curriculum related to Fixed Income
  o   VAR, Black-Scholes, Binomial trees, Greeks, trading strategies, derivative markets

EXPERIENCE
2005 – Present

DEF Trading & Marketing   New York, NY
Work in the Risk Management Group.
• Take lead in developing model in Excel VBA that calculates dollar duration and market value exposures by various categories (i.e. rating, duration, price, etc.) for all municipal portfolio managers within DEF.
• Responsible for calculating monthly performance attribution for all thirty nine municipal funds within DEF.
• Analyze each tax-exempt fund on a monthly basis and identify areas in which a fund is potentially overexposed, in addition to alerting senior management to significant movements in the fund that require attention.

Summer 2004

GHI Corporation   Dallas, TX
Treasury Intern
• Reduced idle cash balances by $79 million, leading to interest expense savings of $2.5 million
• Completed a comparative pricing study on $25 million of commercial banking services
• Revised the design of a cash management Access database containing 6,000 entries

July 2004

JKL, L.L.P. - Financial Advisory Services   Dallas, TX
Junior Leadership Program
• Attended a two day conference with 50 sophomore business students from around the nation

Summer 2003

MNO Securities   Houston, TX
Stock Brokerage Intern
• Developed and generated 1,700 marketing packets for potential clients
• Consolidated 250 clients' investment preferences and risk tolerances into an ACT database

ACTIVITIES

• MBA Investment Fund, L.L.C - *Financial Analyst Program* (August '03 – May '04)
  o   Presented investment strategies to managers of a $10 million equity investment fund
  o   Conducted fundamental analyses and valuations on publicly traded equity securities
• VWX Fraternity of North America – Vice President (Fall '04), Pledge Educator (Spring '05)
  o   Developed & implemented a fundraising campaign with alumni & professional fundraisers – annual contributions have increased from zero to four thousand dollars
• YZA Educational Foundation scholarship recipient

SKILLS

Computer
Bloomberg, Excel, Access, Word, Power Point, ACT, Quickbooks, LIM, Auto-Cad

E

Resumes

CANDIDATE CRITERIA	•Interest in the markets, interest in trading, "PSD" (p.34) •1-2 years experience

Sample Job

COMPANY PROFILE	Strong-performing NYC multibillion dollar event driven hedge fund.
JOB DESCRIPTION	The firm seeks a Junior Trader. The Junior Trader will be responsible for maintaining the trade blotter, executing on trades throughout the day and working on trade confirmation, trade booking and settlements.
JOB REQUIREMENTS	•MUST HAVE 1-2 years prior trading experience at a hedge fund, asset management firm or investment bank •MUST have a bachelors degree from a top tier university •MUST DEMONSTRATE strong interest in public sector investing
COMPENSATION	Competitive base plus bonus

E | Resumes

STRONG POINTS	● **Trading experience**
	● **Trading system skills**
	● **Personable characteristics**

Calvin Coolidge
Address
Phone numbers (home/cell), (work)
email

EDUCATION

ABC University
Bachelor of Science in Economics, *cum laude*, May 2004
- Cumulative GPA 3.6/4.0
- Major in Finance
- XYZ National Honor Society, University Chapter
- ABC University Varsity Lightweight Crew 2002

EXPERIENCE

DEF, LLC, New York, NY, 2004 – 2005
Assistant Trader
- Responsible for the execution of equity orders for senior traders through the SuperDot, Bloomberg, REDI, Instinet and floor brokers on the NYSE, AMEX, and CBOT
- Researched the technicals and fundamentals of all positions on a daily basis (First Calls, Conference Calls, Technical Analysis, etc.) and maintained the P/L and positions for senior traders
- Create daily risk reports for the head trader

LARGE INVESTMENT BANK, New York, NY, Summer 2003
Nasdaq, Assistant Trader-Capital Markets Summer Analyst
- Assisted senior traders in the execution of order flow
- Responsible for timely and appropriate execution of all orders

SMALL MANUFACTURING COMPANY, Corporate Headquarters, Philadelphia, PA, Summer 2002
Financial Analyst Intern
- Evaluated companies' abilities to financially meet firm's requirements for partnership through ratio analysis and an examination of audited financial bidder information
- Updated firm's corporate finance managers on regulatory issues relevant to the industry

SMALL LAW FIRM, Philadelphia, PA, 1998-2001
- Responsible for updating judgment fees and attorney fees for all active files for 20,000 active files
- Organized internal and external meetings for firm partners

ADDITIONAL INFORMATION

- Series 7
- Fluent in Spanish, proficient Salsa dancer
- Study Abroad: Seville, Spain, 2002
- Avid NBA fan

STRONG POINTS	• **Trading experience** • **Trading system skills** • **Simple, clean format**

Adrienne Johnson

Address
Phone numbers (home/cell), (work)
email

Experience

LARGE HEDGE FUND, LLC.   New York, New York
U.S. Equity Junior Trader, June 2003 – Present
- Monitor equity price movements and news for portfolio consisting of 30-40 names
- Troubleshoot and monitor for errors in automated trading system
- Update dividend information for all names in portfolio
- Communicate with operations group to resolve trade discrepancies and settlement issues
- Generate daily P&L and reconcile differences between desk estimated P&L and that calculated by operations

LARGE INTERNATIONAL BROKERAGE FRIM   New York, New York
U.S. Options Junior Trader, May 2002 - May 2003
- Placed stock orders with brokers at market close to keep the open position delta neutral
- Explained large implied volatility movements by keeping daily market journals accessible to senior trader
- Designed spreadsheets for comparison of desk vega position versus benchmark index and analysis of implied volatility versus widely used market ratios
- Communicated with operations group to resolve trade discrepancies and settlement issues
- Reconciled differences between desk estimated P&L and that calculated by the controllers

Large Securities Firm   Boston, MA
Summer Sales Assistant, Intern, Summer 2001
- Organized meetings between analysts, salesmen, and clients
- Assumed liaison role between research analysts and institutional portfolio managers
- Prepared daily research, news, and administrative information for Equity sales force

Retail Firm, New York, NY   Boston, MA
Summer Sales Assistant, Summer 1998, 1999, Summer 2000
- Sell women's sportswear at specialty retailer store
- Exceeded sales expectations by facilitating monthly sales of nearly $10,000 over three month period in Summer 2000
- Helped manage point of sale promotional displays to maximize consumer impact

Skills and Qualifications

Trading System: Reuters, Instinet OMS, and Globex Trader
Computer: Advanced Excel and Bloomberg
Registration: Series 7, 63, and 55
Language: Proficient in Italian

Education

ABC University   Boston, MA
B.A. in *Business Economics,* received May 2002 (GPA 3.4/4.0)
- Coxswain, Heavyweight Men's Crew, 2000-2002

Resumes

E

STRONG POINTS	● **Trading experience** ● **Trading system skills** ● **Leadership experience**

Andrew Johnson
Address
Phone numbers (home/cell), (work)
email

EDUCATION

ABC University, Boston, MA, 2002
Bachelor of Arts: Double Major in Economics and English
Graduation Date: December 2000; GPA: 3.5/4.0

WORK EXPERIENCE

DEF, L.P., Boston, MA   May 2003-Present
Research Trader, Risk Arbitrage Fund
- Responsible for researching corporate transactions including mergers, acquisitions, exchange offers, holding companies, spin-offs, and share classes for investment in resulting equity spreads
- Listen to and summarize corporate conference calls including earnings reports and economic data reports
- Find and employ a variety of outside sources to assist in investment decisions, including Daily Deal, SNL Financial, Brokerage Research, and specialized consulting corporate and legal consulting firms
- Execute trades at the request of portfolio managers

GHI, Investment Banking Division, New York, NY   July 2002-May 2003
Analyst, Financial Sponsors Group
- Prepared industry overview, segmented market analysis, and valuation analysis for pitch books
- Modeled financial scenarios for leveraged buyouts and initial public offerings
- Assessed the suitability of potential acquisition and divestiture targets for private equity portfolio companies
- Maintained firm client coverage and responsibility of JKL

JKL Venture Capital, New York, NY   June 2001-August 2001
Summer Intern
- Responded to client inquiries regarding portfolio performance, term structures, and payout schedules
- Attended meetings with management teams to discuss business and operational strategy and ongoing funding initiatives
- Used discounted cash flow models to value private companies in order to screen investment possibilities

PQR, Consulting & Quantitative Analysis Practice, Philadelphia, PA   January 2000-August 2000
Intern
- Conducted, analyzed and planned transfer pricing methodology and practices
- Provided research assistance and programming support for economic impact studies

LEADERSHIP EXPERIENCE

Young Professionals of Boston, *General Member*   August 2002-Present
XYZ fraternity, Risk-management chairman   August 2000-2002
ABC University Student Association, *Selected by ABC University Student Senate*   September 1997- May 2001

CERTIFICATIONS & SKILLS

- NASD certified Series 7 & Series 63 licensed
- Extensive working knowledge of Microsoft Excel, Word, Access, Power Point, Lexis Nexis, Compustat, Bloomberg, proprietary trading system

F

CAREERS

Those who are drawn to hedge fund analyst and trader positions typically enjoy the public markets and working on the principal side in the heart of the capital markets where they can make or execute educated guesses on the direction of the markets and/or particular equities. They are not limited only to profiting from upswings; they can profit from downswings as well. Meanwhile, the financial compensation for being right and for executing well can be very rewarding.

Those already working at hedge funds, when asked what they most like about their work, often mentioned at least one of the following industry characteristics: meritocratic and refreshingly nonpolitical; the ultimate capitalist opportunity where you find the brightest investors and where individual performance is very transparent; an unbeatable compensation and work/lifestyle situation that is better than in any other area of finance or consulting when a fund performs well.

Usually within three or four years, employees demonstrating their investment acumen will make their mark, unlike comparable employees in investment banks where the road to investment banking success can take a decade, or in large Fortune 500 companies where the road to corporate success can take decades.

FAQ 5 → What Is a Typical Career Path?

Candidates often ask what a career track at a hedge fund looks like. The first thing to note is that career tracks at hedge funds are much less organized and structured than on the sell side or in business in general, and there are fewer title and level distinctions. Analysts typically stay in their role for two to four years, after which they are either promoted to a senior analyst level title—if such a level exists—or a portfolio manager level title, if all goes well. Titles are simply indicators of the level of direct input into the final investment decision-making and allocation process. A senior analyst role is similar to a junior portfolio manager role, and candidates usually are in this role for one to three years.

Execution traders typically remain traders for many years and become senior traders after five plus years unless they reposition themselves for a trader role with P&L responsibilities. Whether or not an execution trader can be repositioned as a trader with P&L responsibilities is left to the discretion of the PM and is very much a function of the individual's aptitude and perceived capabilities and risk management skills.

FAQ 6 → How Stable Is a Hedge Fund Career?

Candidates also ask about the level of stability of a hedge fund job/career. A career can be stable or unstable, depending on the size of the firm and the performance of the firm—often variables beyond the candidate's control. Small firms do not have the financial resources to withstand several consecutive years of bad performance, especially since management fees (1%-2% of assets under management) may not be sufficient to maintain the firm personnel and infrastructure costs. In poorly performing years, not only do hedge funds not earn any profit/fees other than management fees, but they typically cannot earn any future fees outside of management fees until such time as the fund has returned to investors all investor capital lost to date ("highwater mark"). Some PMs have remarked on the potentially unstable aspects of this business model, especially for firms that produce small management fees and firms that do not maintain reserves from good years in the event of difficult times.

Individual performance can also make a career stable or unstable, especially as compared to other finance professions where there is less immediate transparency in the results of individual investment decisions or analyses. Fortunately, most established funds are very good at interviewing and screening candidates before making a hiring decision, and so a personal strategy/style mismatch is much more the one-off exception than the norm. In general, some key mismatch with a new hire in terms of strategy/style becomes obvious within the first 60-90 days of employment, and within 12-24 months, the firm can determine whether there is a good overall fit.

Often if the investing fit or some aspect of the front-office culture fit is lacking, the PM may suggest other opportunities within the fund. As firms develop their infrastructure and become more institutionalized, interesting opportunities emerge in business development, in compliance, in CFO- and COO-level opportunities, and in noninvesting related research at the industry, sector, or macroeconomic level. The trader and analyst roles are only two functional roles within hedge funds. Increased regulation and institutional investor pressure for increased financial management and internal controls have spurred the search for more sophisticated and experienced infrastructure personnel.

A career at a hedge fund can be very stable and lucrative if a fund is performing well and an employee is performing well. Remember that hedge funds never want a strong performer to leave the firm and there is neither a pyramid structure mentality nor an MBA track mentality at hedge funds, making such positions in some sense more stable and meritocratic than more

F Careers

traditional finance positions for younger candidates.

Finally, for any candidate looking for a hedge fund opportunity, it is important to make sure the firm one chooses to associate with is building toward a future. The hedge fund industry is still relatively young—most hedge funds have not had more than a 20-year track record—and the emergence of hedge funds as fully developed organizations with general partners training the next generation of investment professionals is relatively new. You must feel confident that the general partner, typically the founder(s), is looking beyond the length of his/her career(s).

Career stability can also depend directly on the GP/founder's business skill set and his/her motivation in having entered the business to begin with. In terms of skill set, some founders manage money well; some manage people well and know how to build and scale a business; and a subset manage money, people, and organizations well. In terms of motivation, some founders, for example, are motivated primarily by money as a benchmark of success. If this is the case, it is of course important to know how much, as one hedge fund employee recently learned when the founder had reached the $100 million level and was then rarely seen at the office. Others are motivated by a combination of money and intellectual challenge, some purely by ego, some by wanting to build a business that will grow and flourish well beyond the founder's years.

FAQ 7 → What If I Find the Job Is Not for Me?

Some candidates have asked about people who are successful at their hedge fund jobs but ultimately decide that a hedge fund job is not the right career decision. Note that these cases are quite rare. For such candidates, the first line of questioning and self-evaluation should begin by asking whether the real issue is the culture and investment style of their particular employers, not determining whether the hedge fund industry is right for them. For instance, we have noticed analysts at momentum-based shops who end up happier at value funds and vice versa. We have found that when issues do arise they relate mostly to this culture and investment style fit or else to personal investment or trading performance.

The next line of questioning should be about the right functional role with that fund. Although the media and most industry trackers simply monitor the amount and growth of capital allocated to the hedge fund industry, equally significant is the evolution of the funds as organizations, from small, relatively front-office-heavy start-ups (analysts, traders) to more balanced, well-run organizations with personnel in marketing/investor relations, finance, day-to-day operations, technology, business development, compliance, risk management, legal, and human resources. These infrastructure groups, however, still tend to be leanly and efficiently staffed, even at the largest funds. A candidate interested in managing a business rather than managing or trading money should investigate such opportunities.

Once an analyst or trader is certain he/she wants to change industries altogether, there are other opportunities outside of hedge funds, especially in finance or wherever rigorous financial analysis is expected or respected. But it is important to be associated with a firm that does in fact respect and implement a rigorous analysis or trading philosophy. Some momentum-based shops that perform only very routine financial analysis do not prepare candidates for other job opportunities in finance as much as those that are rigorous in their analysis and adhere to high standards in trade execution and risk management. Other types of firms that often seek candidates with hedge fund experience include funds of hedge funds (example: analyst, marketing, operations roles) and hedge fund service providers (example: prime brokerage groups, capital introductions groups, independent research firms, recruiting firms). Both types of firms/groups are experiencing large growth and expansion.

Careers

F

G

COMPENSATION

We will now review compensation for hedge fund analysts and traders. To do so, we must first review some key facts about the nature of hedge fund compensation.

DRIVERS OF COMPENSATION

As a general rule, compensation for analysts and traders in their first few years at an established hedge fund is a function of four factors:

1. **years of relevant experience**
2. **fund performance**
3. **individual performance**
4. **size of the fund (assets under management)**

Meanwhile, location usually affects only base salaries, not bonuses, as the hedge fund industry quickly develops into a national labor marketplace with hedge funds clustered in several key states across the country: New York, Connecticut, Texas, California, and Massachusetts. As portfolio managers groom talented analysts or traders, they also try to provide incentives in the form of financial remuneration, among other things, to encourage these rising stars to stay with the firm.

It should be noted that all four factors mentioned above are interrelated and inseparable. For instance, years of relevant experience (1) must be combined with individual performance (3) for compensation to rise significantly. Simply put, seniority is less a factor in the making of a star employee or partner than meritocracy.

Compensation at the nonsenior levels is usually subjective in the sense that it is based on an annual review and not some formulaic payout, though the presence of what is now becoming a national labor marketplace has created ranges that hedge fund professionals can expect to earn at established hedge funds, again, based on the four factors mentioned above.

SOURCES OF COMPENSATION

How do employees at funds get paid? Their income comes from one of two sources: either from the *management fee* or from the *performance fee,* or *carry.*

For established funds, compensation at the nonsenior level usually comes from the "management fee" of the fund. Some firms also maintain a direct expense account instead of or

Sources of Hedge Fund Employee Compensation — Table 10

I. **Management Fee:** Hedge funds charge their investors or Limited Partners (LPs) a management fee based on a percentage of assets under management. This fee, typically 2% of assets under management, covers most of the personnel costs of the firm other than the senior manager bonuses, which are typically derived directly from the performance fee.

II. **Performance Fee / "Carry":** Hedge fund managers are rewarded primarily in proportion to the profitability (P&L) of the fund's investments. Funds managing LP money typically earn 20% of profits generated. For smaller funds, most personnel depend primarily on the performance fees for their compensation, as management fees are not sufficient to cover these costs.

For hedge fund managers managing internal (General Partnership) capital, there is no such thing as a performance fee, as the capital belongs to the partners of the firm.

III. **Direct Expense Account:** Some firms also maintain a direct expense account *instead of or in addition to a management fee.* This direct expense simply charges investors for all expenses incurred by the hedge fund.

Investor Base		Management Fee	Performance Fee	Direct Expense (if applicable)
	Outside (LP) Investors:	1-3% of assets under management, typically 2%	20% of the P&L, as high as 30%. Manager Comp: 20% -50% of *performance fee*, as high as 60% of fee	ALL COSTS
	Internal (GP) Investors:	NOT APPLICABLE	NOT APPLICABLE Manager Comp: 15% -50% of profit	NOT APPLICABLE

in addition to a management fee. This direct expense simply charges investors for all expenses incurred by the hedge fund, which could either be less than, equal to, or greater than the standard management fee percent of assets structure.

At smaller funds, bonus compensation is derived from performance fees, as management fees are usually enough to cover base salaries. As a result smaller funds may provide analysts a portion of the performance fee or *carry* in the fund **(Table 10).** It is interesting to note that the highest payouts recorded **(Table 11**, see Max column) for analysts with fewer than three years of experience come from funds with approximately $300 million or less in assets.

At the senior level, for those analysts or traders with P&L responsibility, the equation is generally much simpler: Compensation is based on a percent of the carry and is formulaic. In those instances in which it is not formulaic, subjective bonus compensation is usually within a market range. It should be noted, however, that many hedge funds can expose senior analysts and PMs to "netting risk," a scenario in which a strong performer may not be paid as much as expected in a given year if the rest of the firm performs poorly. Candidates should be made aware of such situations prior to accepting a position.

Some firms also offer a percent of the management fee to the manager to allow him/her to pay for staff and resources. As a result, such managers are essentially entrepreneurs within a large firm and must manage their budgets effectively.

Some firms also try to integrate their personnel by allowing managers to participate in overall firm performance. Typically the bulk of a manager's compensation comes from his/her performance. And when one understands the fee structure of a fund, it becomes obvious that the larger the sum of money a manager manages (capital allocation), the greater the likelihood that his payout will be larger.

PAYOUT

Most payouts in the first one to two years are in the form of cash with the option in many instances to reinvest a portion of bonus in the fund. As total cash compensation grows and employees become more integrally involved with the investment decisions process, many funds institute vesting programs as an employee retention plan. Vesting programs are by no means the norm. Other funds have not instituted such programs, nor do they intend to.

For those firms that have embraced such programs, we typically see vesting that can last anywhere from one to three years and can affect from 15% to 40% of an employee's bonus or even higher for more senior compensation. Some of these reinvestment programs and vesting programs can be tax advantageous for employees.

THE NUMBERS

Next we review annual cash compensation levels for hedge fund analysts and traders with little to no experience in investing or trading in public companies. Again, most analysts and traders have had other full-time work experience, making them "experienced" hires. Analysts typically have 3-6 years of full-time work experience. Junior analysts and traders at hedge funds typically have 1-2 years of postcollege work experience.

COMPENSATION: Experienced Analysts and Traders · Table 11

Analysts: 0-1 yrs

BASE SALARY	Sample	Average	Median	Max	Min
2005	16	$105,000	$105,000	$150,000	$75,000
2004	14	$105,000	$100,000	$150,000	$75,000
2003	24	$104,375	$100,000	$200,000	$75,000
2002	16	$98,438	$87,500	$200,000	$75,000
BONUS	Sample	Average	Median	Max	Min
2005	15	$90,000	$75,000	$250,000	$20,000
2004	11	$81,000	$70,000	$250,000	$0
2003	16	$77,875	$72,500	$250,000	$0
2002	16	$77,875	$72,500	$250,000	$0

Analysts: 1-3 yrs

BASE SALARY	Sample	Average	Median	Max	Min
2005	23	$110,000	$110,000	$200,000	$85,000
2004	27	$107,500	$100,000	$200,000	$75,000
2003	44	$105,341	$100,000	$160,000	$50,000
2002	60	$105,667	$100,000	$200,000	$45,000
BONUS	Sample	Average	Median	Max	Min
2005	23	$145,000	$110,000	$900,000	$30,000
2004	21	$141,000	$100,000	$800,000	$0
2003	55	$131,818	$60,000	$900,000	$0
2002	55	$131,818	$60,000	$900,000	$0

Execution Traders: 0-1 yrs

BASE SALARY	Sample	Average	Median	Max	Min
2005	9	$65,000	$65,000	$85,000	$55,000
2004	9	$64,500	$62,000	$80,000	$50,000
2003	6	$59,176	$60,000	$70,000	$50,000
2002	7	$67,857	$60,000	$125,000	$50,000
BONUS	Sample	Average	Median	Max	Min
2005	8	$60,000	$25,000	$180,000	$20,000
2004	8	$61,000	$20,000	$190,000	$0
2003	3	$61,667	$10,000	$175,000	$0
2002	3	$61,667	$10,000	$175,000	$0

Source 1: For 2003 bonus compensation data and for all 2004 and 2005 compensation data, Schwab Enterprise, LLC

Source 2: For data from 2002 to 2003 (base): The Hedge Fund Compensation Report; Institutional Investor, TASS Research, Glocap Search, July 2003 and October 2004

G | Compensation

YEARS 0-1

The first full year at a hedge fund is usually considered a get-to-know-you period for most analysts and traders. Candidates should view the first year as an apprenticeship year. Bonus compensation levels tend to grow quickly after the first year once the hedge fund manager feels comfortable with the aptitude and investment or trading style of the analyst or trader.

Our data indicates that analysts with no more than one year of public sector buy-side experience usually earn about $105,000 in base salary **(Table 11)**. Note that analyst base salaries tend not to rise significantly with experience, while bonuses do. Smaller firms tend to pay first-year analysts a base salary in the high five-figure range, and larger, more established firms pay in the low six-figure range. Bonuses can be as low as 0% of base salary if the firm and/or candidate is performing poorly and as high as 250% of base in a year in which both the firm and the candidate are performing well. The average and median analyst bonus figures lay somewhere in the 70% -100% of base salary range.

Traders typically earn a lower base salary, usually in the mid- to high five-figure range, and bonuses can range anywhere from 0% to 300% , with the average and median bonus figures usually up to 100% of base salary in the first year.

According to Stanford University's Graduate School of Business *2005 Employment Report* **(Table 12)**, recently minted MBAs can expect a base range in the neighborhood of $70,000 to $150,000. Some firms provide a sign-on bonus that can range from $10,000 to $30,000. Although Stanford's compensation data is the only data that explicitly separates hedge fund from asset management compensation data, its numbers are representative within a 15% range of the market for top-tier MBA graduates.

Junior analysts and traders typically earn salaries in line with those of their sell-side counterparts. For example, junior and entry-level analysts from top undergraduate college programs earn a base salary of $50,000 to $65,000, in line with 1st-year investment banking salaries. Junior analysts with two years of postcollege experience typically earn a base salary of $70,000 to $80,000.

Junior level traders start off with a base salary of $35,000 to $50,000. Junior traders with two to three years of postcollege experience typically earn a base salary of $60,000 to $80,000.

YEARS 1-3

Base salaries for experienced hires with 1-3 full years of experience range from $100,000 to $150,000, with the high end of the range reserved for larger funds. Typically, in years in which both an established fund and an analyst perform well, total cash compensation reaches the $300,000 and $400,000 range ("3-handle," "4-handle" compensation) for analysts in their second year and can reach the "5-handle" in year three (based on 2004 bonus data). Star employees can even exceed the "5-handle." Note that such figures are lower for junior analysts who typically have had fewer than five years of postcollege experience, even with 1-3 years of hedge fund experience.

Meanwhile, a sizable portion of funds have instituted vesting schedules for a portion of bonus pay, a practice not yet standard among hedge funds but growing in popularity among managers interested in retaining employees.

Execution trader pay does not experience such a rise, as execution traders at their most senior level tend to peak in the $300,000-$500,000 level and only at large funds.

COMPENSATION: MBA Graduates — Table 12

MBA DATA: Stanford Graduate School of Business

Sample Size	Base $ Median	Base $ Range	Signing Bonus $ Median	Signing Bonus $ Range	Other Guaranteed Compensation $* Median	Other Guaranteed Compensation $* Range
Class of 2005						
6% of 378, or 23	125,000	95,000 - 175,000	25,000	7,500 - 30,000	100,000	20,000 - 150,000
Class of 2004						
5% of 381, or 19	100,000	70,000 - 150,000	27,500	10,000 - 30,000	70,000	15,000 - 200,000
Class of 2003						
6% of 361, or 22	82,500	75,000 - 125,000	15,000	5,000 - 30,000	50,000	25,000 - 200,000

*"Other Compensation" includes only guaranteed compensation, including first-year bonus, relocation expenses, education reimbursement. For 2005 data, "Other Guaranteed Compensation" only includes annual bonus.

Source: Stanford Graduate School of Business, 2005, 2004, 2003, Employment Reports.

G Compensation

AUTHOR

About the Author

CLAUDE SCHWAB is the founder and CEO of Schwab Enterprise, LLC, a hedge fund service provider. Prior to founding Schwab Enterprise, Claude ran the Hedge Fund Recruiting Practice of one of the largest alternative asset management recruiting firms in the United States. Claude also raises capital for hedge fund managers in partnership with Broadmark Capital, LLC. Claude has written for several financial publications, including *Bloomberg News*, and his articles have been syndicated to *The Los Angeles Times* and *The Wall Street Journal*. He wrote the first hedge fund compensation report in partnership with Institutional Investor and Tremont/TASS. He is a guest speaker at industry conferences and is often interviewed and quoted on the hedge fund industry and compensation trends.

Claude earned an MBA from The Wharton School of The University of Pennsylvania, an MA from Columbia University, and a BA from The University of Pennsylvania.

NOTES

NOTES

Schwab Enterprise

LEADING HEDGE FUND SERVICE PROVIDER

Specializing in...

Recruiting
Capital Introduction
Media/Research

SCHWAB ENTERPRISE, LLC
590 Madison Avenue, 21st Floor | New York, NY 10022 | 212-521-4022
www.schwabenterprise.com | info@schwabenterprise.com